# Best Android Apps
## The Guide for Discriminating Downloaders

 by Mike Hendrickson
and Brian Sawyer

Beijing · Cambridge · Farnham · Köln · Sebastopol · Taipei · Tokyo

Best Android Apps: The Guide for Discriminating Downloaders
by Mike Hendrickson and Brian Sawyer

Published by O'Reilly Media, Inc., 1005 Gravenstein Highway North, Sebastopol, CA 95472.

O'Reilly books may be purchased for educational, business, or sales promotional use. Online editions are also available for most titles (*http://my.safaribooksonline.com*). For more information, contact our corporate/institutional sales department: (800) 998-9938 or *corporate@oreilly.com*.

**Editor:** Brian Jepson

**Production Editor:** Nellie McKesson

**Cover Design:** Monica Kamsvaag

**Copy Editor:** Emily Quill

**Proofreader:** Genevieve d'Entremont

**Interior Design:** Josh Clark, Edie Freedman, and Nellie McKesson

**Printing History:**
First Edition: April 2010

ISBN: 9781449382551

[TI]

# Contents

# Contents

# Foreword

When I was asked by O'Reilly to write this foreword, I couldn't help but think back some 20 plus years ago to when the first cell phone was introduced. I still remember how amazed I was that you could make a phone call with no wires or boundaries—all you needed was an extraordinarily large antenna.

Twenty years later, we are doing so many remarkable things, from connecting with friends using the GPS on our phone, to updating our status while waiting in line, to scanning a product's barcode to see if we can get it for a lower price. All with devices that look great and are small enough to fit comfortably in our purses and pockets.

Much of this innovation has occurred on the amazing Android™ platform. If you're reading this, you are part of the incredible growth of Android phones and all those great applications. Congratulations!

This is just the beginning. We've seen Android Market grow from some 50 applications when we first launched the T-Mobile® G1® in 2008 to more than *25,000* as I write this, with more added every day.

But with so many applications, Android users are having a hard time discovering the apps that are right for them. As the leader in Android devices, we want to help you uncover the apps that not only fit your life, but also advance your everyday activities.

That's why for T-Mobile customers, we've launched App Pack, featuring applications tailored to our myTouch 3G users, and T-Mobile Top Picks on Android Market that highlight our recommendations for many of the best apps. We're able to select these meaningful applications based on our unique relationships with developers, through which we get early insights into the latest waves of innovation.

It is also why we are so excited about the launch of *Best Android Apps* from O'Reilly Media. Inside, you'll find 235 of the best applications Android has to offer. And in true Android fashion, you can simply scan and download the applications that appeal to you using the QR codes included in the book.

As I look 20 years into the future, I can only imagine where Android devices and applications will be. I don't know about you, but I am excited to be a part of it!

*Cole*

Cole Brodman
*Chief Technology & Innovation Officer, T-Mobile USA*

# Preface

When Google announced the Android operating system in 2007, we started debating whether it heralded the arrival of an open source platform that could finally compete with the best mobile platforms out there. Our logic roughly followed along the lines of, "What's not to love about a phone operating system that will run on all kinds of devices?" Android quickly exceeded all expectations, and is now a serious contender to become the dominant platform for mobile and smart devices. If you are anything like us, you like choice and do not want a "one-size-fits-all" type of phone. Heck, you might want a keyboard on your phone, or maybe a device that looks like a Fender guitar and is specifically suited to musical interests. Android opens up unlimited possibilities to customize your device to behave just how *you* want it. After all, you know best what you want, and Android-based phones give you plenty of options to choose from. We've had our Android phones for more than a year, and we're still discovering and marveling at all the things they can do.

Of course, having a lot of choices can create a bit of a problem too. As of this writing there are more than 25,000 Android apps in the Android Market, and that number is growing rapidly. At the rate things are going, we'll be at 100,000 apps before long. So how can you find the apps you're looking for and avoid getting overwhelmed with the abundance of options? Many of the apps in the Market claim to do the same thing, and if there are only a few reviews, it can be tough to know what to put on your precious device.

The great thing about these phones is that they can do many things at once. After all, multitasking is how we run our lives these days. But you need the right combination of apps to make your powerful device become a productivity tool, entertainment center, communication hub, reference appliance, gaming gadget, and more.

We wrote this book to help you stay ahead of the current. We scoured the Android Market to find the best apps that will make your phone uniquely yours and help make you more productive, creative, and happy. All the apps in this book work on phones running Android 1.5 and above. If you can't find a particular app in the Market, use Google to see whether you can download a copy from the developers' website. This is another nice thing about Android phones: there is no stranglehold on how you get your apps. They are available directly from the developer as well as from the Market.

### How to Use This Book

The best way to use this book is to browse by subject areas that interest you the most. If you'd rather search by name, the QR Code Index lists all the apps in the book, and what pages they're on.

### About the Authors

**Mike Hendrickson** is a writer, editor, and hacker who continually tries to get the most out of technology, whether it's fused into social interactions, health, politics, environment, or everyday life. In his spare time, he cycles, maintains an organic garden, and practices yoga, and finds/listens to all sort of music with the help of his favorite Android app (Shaazam). Follow Mike on Twitter at @mikehatora.

**Brian Sawyer** is an editor for O'Reilly's Head First division. He's also served as lead editor for the company's popular Hacks series, editor for Missing Manuals and Make: Books, and contributing editor to *Craft* magazine. When not writing about technology, he trains for marathons with the help of his favorite Android apps (see page 96). Follow Brian on Twitter at @briansawyer.

# Best of the Best Apps

Your Android-powered phone is a great tool for getting stuff done—if you select the right apps. Choosing the right app for the task at hand is not always straightforward, especially with so many available that do the same thing. If you're reading this book, you're on the right track, and you're ready to find apps without so much trial and error.

For the past two years Google has run an Android Developer Challenge (ADC), in which large sums of money are awarded to developers who build apps determined to be best of breed in various categories. In the two ADC events held so far, more than 250 apps were selected as winners by Android users and a panel of judges.

In this chapter, we'll look at the top 32 apps for 2009. We'll start with the overall winners first, and then move on to the winners of each of the 10 categories: **Education/Reference**, **Entertainment**, **Games: Arcade/Action**, **Games: Casual/Puzzle**, **Lifestyle**, **Media**, **Productivity/Tools**, **Social Networking**, **Travel**, and **Miscellaneous**.

# Best App for Customizing Your Phone

## SweetDreams
**Free**
**Version: 1.6**
**Inizziativa Networks**

You'll sleep like a baby with the Sweet-Dreams app. If (like most of us) you sleep with your phone on, this app allows you to tune your settings specifically to your needs. Want the phone ringer on but the rest of your alerts off? No problem. Want to get SMS messages but no phone calls? You'll have many ways to customize the way your phone alerts you. This is a really cool, complex, yet intuitive app. Enjoy your beauty rest.

**ON THE MOVE:** If you are up past your bedtime and do not want your phone to go into sleep mode, use the motion filter to keep the phone awake as long as you are still moving around. You can even set the sensitivity, so that a small movement like checking your phone for the time in the middle of the night will not deactivate the sleep mode.

**SILENCE PLEASE:** Activate the sound filter found on the Sound tab to make your phone go into sleep mode only if there is a level of silence that you set. SweetDreams periodically checks the noise level, and if it detects sound above the threshold it will deactivate sleep mode. You can customize the threshold to a level so that your snoring or breathing doesn't deactivate the sleep mode; however, talking in your sleep may be another matter!

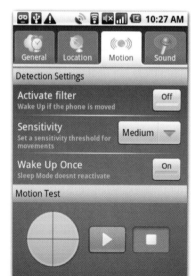

**ON THE SPOT:** The Location tab of the Sweet-Dreams app is pretty straightforward. Simply set your desired sleeping location, and when your phone is in that location it will go into sleep mode. If you are traveling, reset your location by clearing the location list and setting a new activation zone. It's quick, easy, and effective. You can also choose map or satellite views.

**TIME TO SLEEP:** The General tab is where you can set some useful default behaviors. For example, when I'm at home, I silence the ring mode, disable WiFi and Bluetooth, and turn the screen off at 11:30 p.m. I deactivate sleep mode when I begin my day at 5:00 a.m. With the ability to toggle WiFi and Bluetooth on a schedule, this app will save your battery as well as give you peace and quiet!

## Snooze on!

SweetDreams packs a powerful combination of filters to help you sleep even easier. For example, you can set your phone to go into sleep mode when you're in a certain location, not moving around much, and relatively quiet. If even one of these conditions is not met, your phone will stay awake and active. Alternatively, you can set it to go into sleep mode if only one of the conditions is met. It's completely customizable to your personal preference. Sweet-Dreams can also be a lifesaver if you're traveling, particularly when changing time zones. As we've all found out the hard way, even a three-hour time difference can be tough when you've got an early meeting or a late dinner. Tuning your SweetDreams settings can help ease the pain.

# Best Casual Multiplayer Game

## What the Doodle!?
**Free (or $3.99 without ads)**
**Version: 1.0.26**
**Che**

What the Doodle!? is a real-time on-line multiplayer game in which one player sketches out a given phrase and other players guess what it is. It's dangerously addictive, and may lead to doodling during boring meetings. One nice feature is the built-in social networking. You can connect to friends, have a private game where you invite only specific people, or play a random game with the world at large. So next time you're in a yawner of a meeting, get your doodle on.

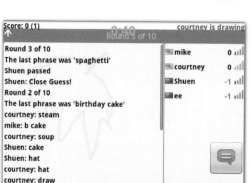

**DOODLER EXTRAORDI-NAIRE:** Make sure to set up your profile well so people can find you—consider using your Twitter, Facebook, IM, or email username. This allows you to set up a friends-only game. Be warned that you're not allowed to draw numbers or letters, or you'll lose the game. Also, make sure you know what you want to draw before you start scribbling. There is no eraser, only a clear button that will wipe out your masterpiece and force you to start over from scratch.

**TAKE ACTION:** Think fast, because you have only 40 seconds to get a winning guess in. Not only that, but there are some sharp players out there who answer within seconds. Draw quickly when your turn comes, because if people aren't getting it, you want as many chances as possible to redraw. Watch out—you lose points if nobody can figure it out!

BIG GUNS: If you dare, challenge the highest-ranked players and see if you have what it takes to play with the big guns. Limited bio information is available for each player. Many of the top players have doodled a picture for their avatar; you can, too, by going to Options→Face Doodle. Finally, if a player gets obscene or offensive with their doodling, you can vote to boot them from the game.

LEADERBOARD: Track your progress with a stats page that shows your rank, how well you guess, and how well you draw. The stats page also shows how many games you have played and won, both individually and as part of a team.

### Got Game?

If you want to challenge your inner circle, you can set up a private, friends-only game and wait for your friends to join. They'll need to know the name of the private game to find it. If you get impatient, press the Home button, send a text message from your SMS app, and return to the game by clicking on the icon in your status bar that this app leaves in place while it's running. For example, I can set up a private game and text a couple of friends with ChompSMS and tell them to get their Doodle on. I let them know that my text name (mikehatora) is the same as my Doodle name so they can find the game quickly. This way, if you have a family event and a couple of Android phones, you can have a nice little "family feud." You can take a screen capture of the image that is drawn by using the menu button.

# Best App for Mobile Security

## WaveSecure

**Free**
**Version: Beta - 3.0.0.40**
**tenCube**

If you're among the 20 million people in the world who lose their phones each year, you'll appreciate the security this app provides. With WaveSecure, you can back up all your data, videos, photos, and other media. If your phone is lost or stolen, you can wipe out all the data remotely, and restore it later if you find your phone. You can also lock down your phone to protect sensitive data that you don't want falling in the wrong hands, like your saved passwords.

**TAKE ACTION**: You've lost your phone! What's your first move? Well, if you've made backups with this app, you can safely go ahead and wipe all the data off the device. Then, you can lock it down completely. In this way, you've not only removed all of your sensitive data, files, and settings, but you've also disabled the device so that no one can even use it. This is pretty slick for thwarting would-be thieves.

**PHYSICALLY LOCKED**: Normally if you lose your phone, someone can just switch out the SIM card and your phone (and data) would be gone. However, with WaveSecure, any attempt to switch out the SIM card would lock down the phone. Not only that, when someone tries to switch the SIM card, the phone will sound an alarm, send you its location, and instruct the holder to call a number and return it. This is high-security stuff!

**WEB SECURE:** WaveSecure's web interface displays all the actions you can run remotely when your device is lost, including Lock, Track, Location, Backup, Wipeout, and Restore. It also lets you view the data that is backed up on the server. You can view contacts, SMS messages, call logs, and media. So even if someone was able to get past your SIM change lock and put in a new SIM card, you would be able to see their call logs, SMS messages, contacts, and media additions.

**LOCATION, LOCATION, LOCATION:** Once logged into the website, you can track your phone's location and set the tracking interval—for example, you can tell WaveSecure to record your phone's location every 60 minutes. Customize your view by selecting one of the four map options: Map, Satellite, Hybrid, or Terrain. Sort by location (to see how many times your phone visited the Starbucks on 9th St, for example), or sort by date to see all the places your phone visited on that particular day. The location page also displays the most recent service provider, so if someone inserts a different SIM card, you'll know which company to contact to find out about recovering your device.

## Secure, Really?

Let's be frank—you're never completely secure if your phone is lost or stolen. In a matter of minutes, I managed to use the Software Development Kit (SDK) to browse the filesystem and access all the data and files on a locked-down phone. And if I can do it so easily, it's a sure bet that someone who makes a living preying on unsuspecting people will get access too (unless there is a setting I missed that prevents access from the SDK file manager). So you need to take precautions. First, back up your system using this app. Then, if you lose your phone, don't just lock it down—wipe it first. Just do it! *Then* lock it down so the phone will send you its GPS coordinates. If it is in your house or another place you know, look harder. And if it is truly lost or stolen, at least you wiped the data so that you won't be financially vulnerable to an unscrupulous thief.

# Best App for Appreciating Art

## Plink Art

**Free**
Version: 1.1.3
plinkart.com

If you like art, share it with the Plink Art app. You can search by using a photo of the work, or by artist name or title. You can also peruse random artwork, view a timeline of art, or check out curated galleries. The attractive interface makes it easy to share, get more information, navigate to Wikipedia for more details, or discuss and make comments on the work. If you want to purchase a poster of the work, one click takes you to allposters.com.

**USE EXISTING PHOTOS:** Searching for art by using a photo or web image works extremely well. For example, I took a picture of one of the cards from the National Gallery of Art's *Close Up Card Game*. Within 10 seconds, Plink Art had identified the work and returned the results to my phone. From there, I could easily share it, discuss it, explore different facets of it, or purchase a poster of it.

**ART HISTORY LIVE:** Exploring the timeline helps bring to life the major art movements of the past. It's a great way to study for your midterm, prepare yourself for a date at the art gallery, or just simply for the joy of learning about art. If you want to explore more, just click Explore and related works by artist, museum, and genre will appear quickly. There are lots of reasons to love this app!

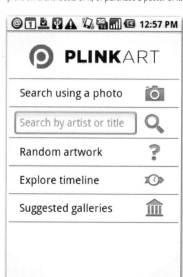

# Best Word Game

## Word Puzzle

**Free**
**Version: 2.0**
**Best App**

This is a great game to challenge your vocabulary and spelling abilities. You are presented with three letters, and you have 30 seconds to create as many words as you can that begin with those letters. Word Puzzle was designed for kids, but it can be addictive and challenging for adults, too.

**ROUNDS OF ACTION:** Each round gives you 30 seconds to complete as many words as you can. Type fast, don't make mistakes, and think about using derivative words to boost your score. In other words, if you get *RUN*, you can make runs, running, runner, rune, runes, runners, rundown, runway, runback, and more before you get to the more difficult words like runcible.

**CHALLENGE YOUR FRIENDS:** Play a round and then pass your phone to a friend (or your kid!) and see if they can beat you. Click on Challenge and automatically see where your score fits on the leader board. The words will repeat after a few games, so don't get too cocky if you start to get high scores. After all, this game was created for young children learning to spell new words!

# Best App to Navigate the Solar System

## Celeste SE

**$1.99**
**Version: 1.0.3**
**Terminal Eleven LLC**

It may be a dark and stormy night, but regardless of whether you can see the stars, this app has you covered. Simply point your phone in any direction and it will place the planets on the screen in accordance with your geographical position. Using this app is pretty simple: the first time you run it, you are prompted to make figure-eight motions to calibrate and coordinate the tracking and GPS. This app is especially cool at night, with all the objects in our solar system visible.

10

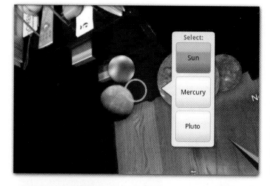

**FIND YOUR DIRECTION AND PLANETS:** If you're at all like me, you may sometimes feel like a bit of an extraterrestrial. Now you can find your place in the universe. As you move your phone around, you will see various heavenly objects super-imposed onto your world. Keep going and find your planets.

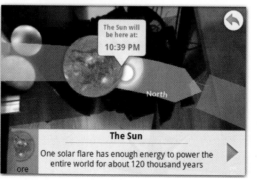

**TRACK:** If you move your phone to a point along the path a planet is going to take, Celeste will indicate when it will reach that point. You will also see the other planets that are in the same trajectory. Click on an object in the solar system to read some interesting facts about it.

# Best Photo Game

## A World of Photo

**Free**
**Version: 1.0.5**
**Michael Elsdörfer**

This is a modern "spin" (ahem) on the old "spin the bottle" game. Everyone is connected through "Central," and from there you will be prompted to spin your phone. The app will move on the map in the direction that the phone stops, and try to find someone for you to send a photo to. Keep in mind that that person will be rating your photo, so try to make it interesting—don't just take a picture of your TV screen (I received one of these)! The more highly rated photos you send, the more your reputation will grow.

**WHAT'S GOING ON:** A World of Photo offers a cool, unique way of seeing what's going on in the world. People exchange photos from different parts of the globe, and each photo reflects that person's individual perspective and environment. Watch out, though—this app can become addictive!

**SPREAD YOURSELF THIN:** Always accept the opportunity to contribute a photo. Make it interesting because people will be rating you. Your stats will show up in Central, which shows the activity across the network (photo sharing and ratings). It's neat to see your photo travel around the world. Suggestion: be nice when rating others' photos. They'll be rating you too.

# Best App for Locating Song Information

## SongDNA
**Free**
**Version: 1**
**Dedicado B.V. & 8Projects**

Go ahead—embrace your inner hippie, rock 'n' roller, pop star, or whatever floats your music boat with this app. Simply search for a song you want to know more about, and voilà—you'll have oodles of information at the tap of your finger. This app does a mash up of data from MusicBrainz, Billboard, lyricsfly, BBC Music, YouTube, BrandsInTown, Twitter, and Google Analytics to bring you the most up-to-date information.

**SIMPLE START:** This app might not look like much when you first fire it up, but hold on—it'll bring back more information than you think. Make sure you pay attention to your search criteria. My first search for find Bob Dylan's "Beyond Here Lies Nothing" went unfulfilled, simply because Nothing is spelled Nothin' in the song title. This app does not have a "Do you mean" feature like Google, so be careful to search for exactly what you want to find.

**MASHUP HEAVEN:** This app mashes up several sources and returns great results in an organized manner. If you're wondering whether the artist has a website, Twitter account, videos on YouTube, Wikipedia page, or any plans to tour in your city, this app can give you all that info in one click. Another cool feature is that lyrics are included, but even cooler, you can fix incorrect lyrics by going directly to lyricsfly.com from this app.

# Best Pocket Guitar App

## Solo
**Free / £1.50 Full version**
**Version: 1.6**
**Coding Caveman**

If you want to play the guitar or if you already do play the guitar, this app will let you practice and perfect your skills. You can highlight a chord from the chord bar on the top and then strum the strings to hear the chord played. Select Instrument from the menu to choose which kind of guitar you want to play. Select Play Music and you can load in your songs or find lyrics and chords from the Internet.

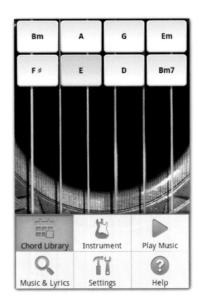

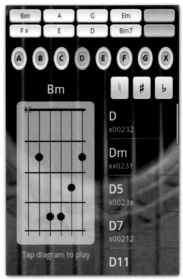

**HEAR THE MUSIC:** After you select the chord you want to play, you can then select different strings to hear what they sound like in that chord. The chord you have selected is highlighted in green, and when you strum the strings, only the strings that are meant to be played in that chord will play. If you crank up the volume, you can even make your own music.

**SEE THE MUSIC:** This app lets you see the chords as well as hear them, which is particularly useful when you're just learning how to play. The black dots indicate where your fingers should be positioned on the strings, and the red X means that no fingers should be depressing that string. You can save your chord layouts and load them at a later time, or load new ones from songs.

# Best 3D Arcade Game App

## Speed Forge 3D
€1.99
**Version: 1.2**
**Rat Square**

Amazing 3D graphics make Speed Forge a truly standout app. It's another addictive game that will have you coming back for more. Note that it's not a game for a boring meeting, however—it's hard to play this one inconspicuously. You maneuver your on-screen hovercraft through the race course by moving your phone around: turn your device to make a turn, tilt down to slow, and tilt up to accelerate. You'll find it dangerously easy to get sucked into this twisting and turning, action-packed game.

**REAL ARCADE FEEL:** Speed Forge feels like a classic arcade game, and even includes vibrations as you scrape the walls of the course. Make fine turns by tilting your device one way or another. Check it out when you have some time to kill, and play a couple of rounds on the free version before you purchase the full version.

**CUSTOMIZE YOUR GAME:** The free version gives you limited ability to customize the game, but the full version has lots of bells and whistles. You can configure how you feel and hear the game as you play it. Be warned, though, that the fancy graphics will drain your battery fast. You may want to plug in your device while you play.

# Best Gravity-Defying Game

## Graviturn Extended
**Free**
**Version: 2.0**
**Florian Heft**

In this game, use gravity to move the red balls off the board while keeping the green ball from falling off the screen. It's simple and there are very few rules, but there are an infinite number of levels to move through as you tilt and move your device to maneuver the balls. This gravity-resisting game will challenge you in different ways, and once you get to level 10, you can tap on the screen and remove blocks that impede your progress. Watch out—this game is addictive!

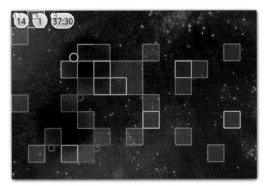

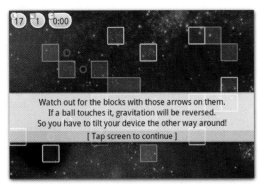

Watch out for the blocks with those arrows on them. If a ball touches it, gravitation will be reversed. So you have to tilt your device the other way around!

[ Tap screen to continue ]

**KNOW YOUR STATS:** This app remembers where you left off, and brings you back to that level when you restart your game. For each level you complete, you will be shown stats on how quickly you completed it and how you compare to others around the world.

**PROGRESSIVE DIFFICULTY:** As you progress through the levels, more and more obstacles will get in your way. Gravity holes, removable blocks, and other items will pop up to spoil your rapid progress. Each level presents new and different challenges. This game is a bit unpredictable as you move on.

# Best Motorbike Game

## Moto X Mayhem

**Free**
**Version: 1**
**Dejan Cecar & Tyler Wilson**

This game is tough but addictive. You tilt and tap the phone to accelerate and navigate your motorbike through the different course levels. The controls are intuitive, with the use of the accelerometer for leaning forward and backward on your bike. Tapping on the left side of the screen brakes. whereas tapping on the right accelerates. You can do flips and stunts, but they have no impact on your score. You can check your top scores and those of other players around the world.

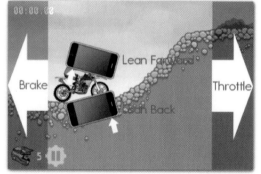

**ACCELEROMETER:** This app uses the phone's accelerometer to allow you to jump forward or lean back. It makes a big difference—for example, when you're going up a hill and lean too far back, you'll tip over and have to start again. You'll need to constantly be aware of your body position when you speed up or slow down. It's a hoot.

**SIMPLICITY RULES:** There are only three settings in Moto X Mayhem—Sound, Music, and Tilt Sensitivity—and there are seven levels of difficulty. So your high score depends on your mastery of tilting and tapping. Go ahead and tilt and tap your way through the levels, and see how you stack up against other players.

# Best Mystery Logic Game

## Totemo
Free Lite / £1.50 Full version
Version: 1.25
Hexage

Ready for a challenge? Check out this game. Once you get to Level 7, this puzzle starts to get difficult, and the difficulty gets more intense with each level. This is a great way to wake up your mind in the morning. Although the main goal (clearing rows or columns of objects) sounds simple, you must clear objects in groups of two, three, or more, which can get tricky. Want to keep your kids occupied while on a long journey? Put this in their hands.

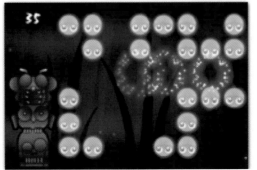

**MIND BENDERS:** At first it might look like you can muddle through this game with trial and error, but you really need to plan out your moves. A brief message tells you how to proceed with each level. Be mindful of what these messages tell you.

**CHALLENGE YOUR FRIENDS:** Have a few of your buddies install this app and see who can finish a level first. Or race your way through three levels at a time. As you figure out the game parameters, Totemo challenges you with new levels. You'll want to grab the full version, because the lite version only goes up to 12 levels.

17

# Best App for Passing the Time

## Mazeness
Free
Version: 2.0
Bogee Int.

Success in this game is dependent on your ability to perform small but firm actions on your phone, like tapping on the side, in order to maneuver the balls around the map. You need to move two balls simultaneously toward the target, which is a gold bull's-eye. As you would expect, the game gets more difficult as you progress through the levels. There are items on the grid that either help or hinder your ability to master the level. This game grows on you quickly.

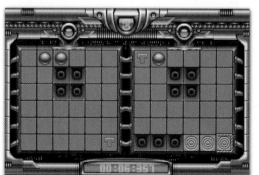

SENSE YOUR WAY AROUND: This game gives you the option of turning the sensor and vibration on or off. I'd suggest turning them both on. This way you get a real, physical sensation as you move the balls around the screen. Turning the sensor and vibration off makes playing the game less visceral but more difficult.

LEFT, RIGHT, UP, DOWN: All you have to worry about are simple directional movements. Easy! But there are also special icons that appear. Some take your ball to different places, and others inhibit your progress. It's maddening and challenging at the same time, and this app keeps you coming back for more.

# Best Augmented Reality Game

## SpecTrek

**Free**
**Version: 1.0.8**
SpecTrekking.com

If you'd like to be a Ghostbuster (or at least pretend you are), you can walk around playing this virtual ghost hunting game. This augmented reality app uses your phone's GPS and camera to overlay gameplay on the real world, so you can hunt for virtual ghosts across a map of where you are. You can also check your awards, game progress, stats, and records. It's like an old-style scavenger hunt, but for ghosts. Who you gonna call?

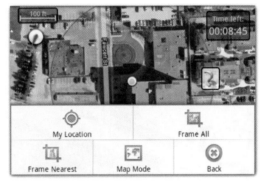

**GHOSTBUSTING LEGEND:** Spec-Trek allows you to create up to three different profiles. You can use them for different locations, times, or even for letting someone else play your copy of the game. I use one profile on the way to work and another at home at night.

**AUGMENT YOUR WORLD:** Face it, augmented reality is really cool, and this app touches just the tip of what is possible. You'll get hooked on looking for ghosts in your surroundings. I find myself walking by "past-finds" and thinking, "Hey, this is where I found ghost #3!" Chase some ghosts around your city, house, or office, and burn some calories while you're at it!

# Best App to Customize Your Ringtone

## FoxyRing

Free
Version: 1.5
LevelUp Studio

Don't let the name of this app confuse you. This context-aware ringtone app lets you set up rules for different locations, so that your phone switches ringtone based on the position reported by your GPS. FoxyRing even filters the sound volume based on the ambient noise in your surroundings. So if you are at a noisy public event, you get a loud ring; if you are in a quiet office, you get a quiet ring. You can also define your sleeping hours to mute your rings while you slumber.

**RING SMART:** The sleep feature is great: you can turn off all rings, data, Bluetooth, and notifications based on your normal sleeping hours. You can also define emergency contacts with a special ringtone that can get through even if you are in a "sleep zone." I find this very useful because I want to make sure my aging parents can reach me whenever they need to.

**PHYSICAL ZONE:** This app not only uses different ringtones for different times of day, but also for different locations. I have my normal ringtone set for my office in Cambridge and louder ringtones when I am at home. This geo-temporal-contextual feature is a great way to customize your phone.

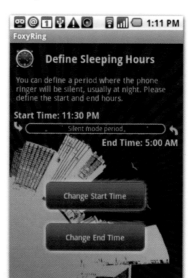

# Best App for Filtering News Information

## Buzz Deck

**Free**
**Version: 1.0.1**
**mippin.com**

With all the different news sources out there, keeping up can be a monumental task. Enter Buzz Deck, an app that aggregates all the different sources into one place. It can bring you CNN, ABCNews, Twitter, Facebook, and any other hotbeds of information about world, national, and local happenings. If you prefer a source that isn't among the built-in offerings, you can add a custom "card" with the web URL—and you can add as many custom cards as you want. Then, fine-tune the app's notification settings to get updates when you want.

**SELECTIONS ABOUND:** This app is an excellent way to manage all your information channels in one place, and it offers a great selection of sources to start with. Just select one of the standard icons, and you'll start to receive the summary information for that category. Note that if your refresh rate is set for only once a day, you may want to refresh manually after you add any new channels.

**CUSTOMIZE TO YOUR HEART'S CONTENT:** If you want to go beyond the standard cards, enter a URL and Buzz Deck loads it. It's like building your own newspaper, one card at a time. I can receive and read news faster through this app than by perusing copies of the *Boston Globe* and the *New York Times*. This is the news of the future.

# Best App for Mobile TV

## SPB TV
**Free / $9.95 Full version**
**Version: 1.1.0**
**SPB Software**

If watching TV in your doctor's waiting room doesn't cut it, give this app a try. SPB TV allows you to take your own TV programs wherever you go. The free "lite" version is shown here, but you'll probably want to splurge for the pay version to get more channels. There's even a picture-in-picture feature, which is handy if you're not sure which program to watch. Obviously, this isn't a full cable-like TV in your pocket—it has limitations, including battery life and bandwidth constraints. But it still beats watching airport TV.

**STOCK PROGRAMS:** There are hundreds of TV shows that are loaded in the pay version of SPB TV. They can be accessed by flicking the icons at the bottom of the window. The show you are considering will pop up, and if you select it, you may be provided with information about upcoming show times. Click on a show time, and you will be prompted to add the time/show to your calendar.

**TV GUIDE:** SPB TV may not quite compare to a full cable package, but it offers a good variety of shows. If you find a show you enjoy, then you can look for future airings on your particular channel. Click on the time and you will be prompted to add it to your calendar. Scroll on the date to move from day to day while still on the same channel.

Current weather conditions for US cities and surrounding areas.

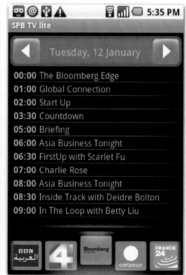

# Best App for Taking Photos w/Effects

## FxCamera
Free
Version: 0.5.4
ymst

This app uses layers to add interesting effects to the photos you take. There are six effects you can use to transform your photo: Normal, Warhol, SymmetriCam, Fisheye, Polandroid, and ToyCam. When using the camera normally, this app will auto-focus for you and give you options to set the quality. You can also choose effects such as Mono, Sepia, Negative, Posterize, or Solarize—you can even take a normal picture! Once you're done, it's easy to save or share your photo.

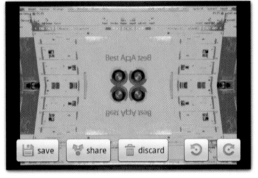

**SUBMENUS:** All of the effects except Warhol have submenus that offer more options to choose from. The config button will take you to these options if they are available. You can get pretty creative and make some neat effects. Take the time to figure out how they work, and you'll have a blast with this app.

**BEAUTY IN THE EYE OF THE BEHOLDER:** This app makes it easy to play around with top-notch photo effects and turn a normal, everyday picture into a work of art. The menus are simple and intuitive, so even an amateur photographer can master this app.

# Best App for Sharing Contacts

## Hoccer

**Free**
**Version: 1.0.2**
**Art+Com Technologies**

Hoccer is not only handy and convenient, but it's also cool to use. You can share data, contacts, or whatever else you want by making gestures similar to throwing a frisbee. It's like playing catch with information, and it's fun and useful with this app. Whether you want to share a contact, picture, bookmark, or text, Hoccer is just right for a quick exchange of data. For example, a speaker at a conference could throw his contact details out to the audience, and people with this app could catch the information.

**CONTACT SHARING:** Why keep all your contacts locked up? Share them with others, and have fun at the same time. Simply fire this app up, select a contact, mimic throwing a frisbee, and voilà—your contact is on its way to a new device. This is so simple, yet ridiculously fun and addicting. You may find yourself walking around looking for opportunities to throw data.

**YOU CAN MAKE IT SECURE:** You probably don't want to share your boss's information with just anyone, so if you want to send info to only one person, you can: tap on your device and you will pair with another user's device; if the user accepts your pairing request, you're connected exclusively. It's not absolute security in a large group setting, but in most cases it's good enough.

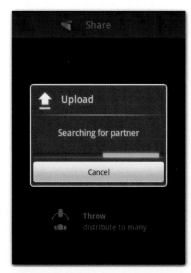

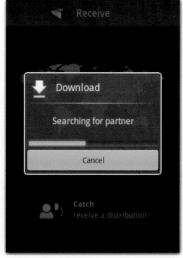

# Best App for Triggering Actions

## Tasker
**Free**
**Version: 1.0.1**
**tasker.dinglisch.net**

Tasker gets to the heart of what makes Android, well, Android—it allows you unrestricted freedom to do anything you want with your apps and your phone. After all, your phone should work for *you*! This app can add extra actions to your settings. With more than 100 actions available in 12 categories—and each action with its own customizable set of parameters—it's hard to believe how much functionality is crammed into one app.

**CUSTOM APP BEHAVIOR:** You'll recall that the SweetDreams app can deactivate sleep mode when it hears a sound louder than breathing or snoring. I take it a step further with Tasker: I want my phone to go into record mode so I can hear what the noise was or listen to myself babble in my sleep. With Tasker, I create a task that starts five minutes after I sleep, waits for SweetDreams to deactivate, and then records. Slick.

**CREATING A TASK:** Tasker offers a bunch of built-in variables to help you create your task. Combine all the options, set your limits, specify threshold conditions, and you've created a task. Use these variables to control what triggers a task and what happens when it's triggered. You can also check out the online tutorial for more help mastering Tasker: *http://tasker.dinglisch.net/index.html*.

# Best App for Spotting Everyday Trends

## Ce:real

Free
Version: 1.0
Neowiz Internet

Ce:real is a visual interface to Twitter and TwitPic, as well as other photo sharing sites that interact with Twitter trends. It takes the most talked-about items from Twitter and mashes them up with pictures from photo sites that have similar tags. Ce:real is a very easy and intuitive app to use, and setup is minimal. There are two main areas to browse: Trends and Public Timeline. You can also search by keywords and find matching pictures and status updates.

**TREND WATCHING:** If you want to see what is happening in the world around you, fire up this app. Ce:real uses Twitter locales to bring back the pics that are related to your search and location. You can also use this app to upload a photo along with your tweet. This app does not filter the images that you might see, so use caution with what you search for.

**DIVE IN:** The pictures that Ce:real finds will appear in little circles on your screen. Click on a circle, and you'll see the tweet that went with the picture; you'll also have the option to save the picture, re-tweet it, or send it as an email. As a Twitter user, you probably don't spend a lot of time looking at the trends and public timeline; this app will keep you up to date on what's happening.

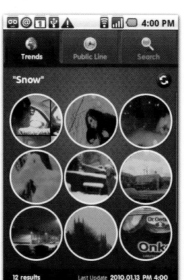

# Best App to Share Your Musical Tastes

## SocialMuse

**Free**
**Version: 1.0.1**
mixzing

If you like to listen to music and discover what other people listen to, this app is for you. In essence, SocialMuse is a peer-to-peer app that lets you browse music libraries, preview music, and get useful information on songs that interest you. You also get to learn a little bit about people who are sharing music of similar taste. It's easy to set your preferences. Simply type in your favorite musicians, and the app autocompletes the name.

DISCOVERY: To see who's listening to what kind of music, you can filter by gender, age, and location. I like to go to the map, zoom out, and see what's going on in Europe. I typically find interesting music on phones far away. And as more people get Android phones around the world, this app will get better and better.

BROWSE SOMEONE'S LIBRARY: Once you find someone who is using SocialMuse and sharing music, you can connect to them and browse through their library. If you click on a song, you can choose to play a song preview, buy the song (Amazon mp3), or go to YouTube, Google, or Wikipedia for information about the song. This is peer-to-peer music on your phone.

# Best App for Finding a Specific Spot

## SpotMessage

Free
Version: 2.5.0
Vanpool Co., Ltd.

This app allows you to remind yourself or others of something of interest (or something to do) at a certain location. For instance, I typically get gas for my car on Mondays because one of our local stations has an 8 cents per gallon discount that day. Now, instead of blithely driving by in a preoccupied haze, I can have a message sent to me when I'm getting close to remind me to stop in. This is the essence of spot messaging: go by a spot, and receive a message.

**HOME IN:** To make this work well, you need to know your location, at least at the street level. Once you pick the street, you can narrow the radius by using the minus sign. Then it's just a matter of clicking the placement icon to mark your spot. The radius is fairly wide, which accounts for imperfect GPS reception. If you already know where you need to go, the reminder is all you need to jog your memory.

**SHARE YOUR SPOTS:** You have the option to share your spots with friends via Twitter, Delicious, Facebook, text message, email, and QR Codes (two-dimensional barcodes). For example, you could send your friends a "stop for a beer" message. This would help your friends who might not be familiar with your local establishments. I think this app has tons of potential, especially for memory-challenged folks.

# Best App for Chronicling Your Trips

## Trip Journal

**Free / €1.99 Full Version**
**Version: 1.3.0**
**iQapps**

If you are going on a trip, use this app to keep a journal. The menus and selections are well laid out and self-explanatory, and the map and satellite views make it easy to spot your waypoints. This app is full of features, including statistics (speed, time, altitude, etc.), photo journaling, writing notes, managing waypoints, tracking your route, and locking your screen so your journal does not get messed up. You can even reverse your tracks with one click, which is great for finding your way back home.

**TRIPPIN' AWAY:** Even if the free time on your journey consists of five-minute intervals, you can still create a memorable journal of your travels. Simply snap a photo, add a note, add it to your waypoint, and later export it to Google Earth. Each of these activities will be encoded with your current GPS location so you can get a true picture of where you are in the world. The menus have great navigation and are graphically appealing.

**SHARE THE TRIP:** One nice feature of Trip Journal is its export capability. You can export your journal to Picasa, Flickr, or Facebook, as well as to KMZ (for Google Earth). When you set up the app, you'll choose which email address you want exports to go to. Once you export to Google Earth (which requires only one click), you can open up all the activities that you recorded along the way; Google Earth will move you to each waypoint and provides statistics on time elapsed, distance traveled, speed, altitude, and latitude and longitude. You can choose whether to use metric or imperial measurements in the settings menu.

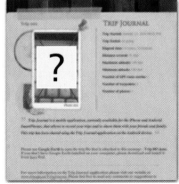

# Best App for Location-Based Alerts

## iNap: Arrival Alert
**Free**
**Version: 1.0.0**
**Moop.Me**

The idea of iNap is pretty simple: get on your bus or train, set an alert for a particular destination point, and settle down for a nap. When you arrive within the radius of the destination that you set earlier, you'll be awakened by your phone. If you've ever snoozed past your stop and had to muddle your way home, you know exactly how useful this app can be. You could also use this app on a trip to make sure you don't miss points of interest along the way.

**TAKE AIM:** Click to open your destination point, and you'll see a map that you can focus in on by using the + and - signs after you tap the screen. You will be able to review your trip before you set it as final and start your nap. This is a good app for long-haul travel, especially if you need to catch up on sleep before taking your turn driving.

**REMEMBER YOUR LOCATIONS:** This app keeps track of your arrival destinations as you add them. I only save locations that I might want to wake up at, like South Station in Boston after a late-night train ride from NYC. I set my alert to vibrate 30 minutes before arrival, so I can snooze in the quiet car and still get woken up if I fall asleep with my noise-canceling headphones on.

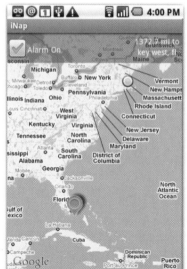

# Best App for Locating Your Car

## Car Locator
**Free trial / $3.99 Full version**
Version: 2.50
Edward Kim

Have you ever parked in a huge parking lot, say, at a sporting event, concert, or some public celebration like the Fourth of July? And did you then find yourself wandering around endlessly looking for your car? This app remembers where you parked and gives you directions back to your car. There's also a space where you can add notes, such as "row H3 on Third Level of Public Parking Garage on Main Street." This is a handy app.

**PINPOINTING YOUR WHEREABOUTS:** When you park your car, all you have to do is click Menu and then Save Location. Then you're free to enjoy your activity without having to worry that you'll be wandering in circles afterward. The radar graph will show you where you are and where you need to go. You can use map or satellite views; the satellite view shows detail you may need to find your way.

**AVOID PARKING VIOLATIONS:** The Car Locator app also allows you to track how long you've been parked. This is handy if you're parked at a parking meter; you can set the app to notify you when your time is about up. In addition, the direction arrows will help you get to your car quicker. In this view, the distance is prominently displayed, much larger than on the radar view.

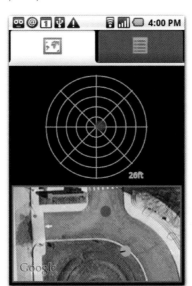

# Best App for Composing Guitar Music

## Rhythm Guitar

$1.00
Version: 1.3.0
sotap

The Rhythm Guitar app is based on three main activities: playing chords, creating/editing chords, and creating/editing progressions. Progressions are series of chords that are the building blocks of songs. The simulated guitar has six strings and five frets clearly displayed, with the top fret representing the head of the instrument. There are two ways to play a chord: when you select it from the list, or when the program first fires up and the name of the current chord is displayed in the middle of the screen.

**LEARN THE CHORDS:** This is a great way to practice chords for those of us just learning (or perpetually learning) to play the guitar. It is one thing to hear music, and another to read and play the music. I particularly like the fact that I can go at my own pace and then try it out on a real instrument. Make this the year you finally learn to play the guitar—this app is a great place to start.

**CREATE YOUR OWN CHORDS:** This is a bit beyond me at the moment, but I can use this app to create new chords. (Whether anyone else wants to hear them is another matter.) The creator/editor is very easy to use, and you can put together a bunch of chords into a progression quickly. The progression editor is straightforward, and includes samples so you can see how a progression is composed.

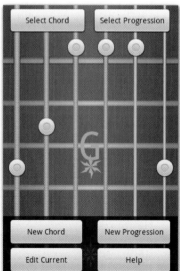

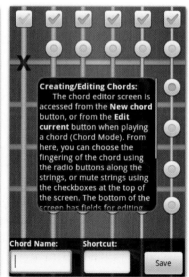

# Best App to Determine Object Distance

## Andrometer

**Free**
**Version: 1.0.3**
**Highway North Interactive, Inc.**

Have you ever wondered how far it is to that house you see on the top of the hill? Or how far you'd have to swim to make it across the lake? Andrometer allows you to measure the approximate distance between you and an object, or the height and width of something you see on the horizon. So how tall is that building you always see on your way to work? You can get a pretty good approximation by installing Andrometer.

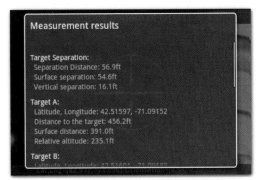

**MEASURE IT:** This app works best if you you are outside where there is good GPS reception. If you want to measure the width of a building, simply click on Width, take a snapshot of one corner of the building, then walk 20 meters and snap the other corner. The accelerometer and geomagnetic sensor will do the calculations for you.

**DETAILS OR SUMMARY:** Once you measure something, you can view either the details or the summary of that item. I like to see both, and fortunately they are only a click away. This app is better for measuring larger objects like buildings, rather than smaller, up-close objects.

# Best App to Simulate a Golf Caddy

## GPSCaddy
**Free / £12.99 Full version
Version: 2.5.0
Calton Hill**

If you golf, the GPSCaddy app is for you. Purchase the full version so you can access all the maps and have all the features unlocked. This app gives you awesome views of the hole you are playing, and uses GPS to tell you precisely how far away you are from the hole, trees, water, and sand traps. You can download course maps from the Calton Hill Golf website (*www.caltonhillgolf.com*). Just plug in your city and state, and the app lets you choose your courses.

**IN YOUR POCKET:** I've always hated keeping score of my golf games; I despise the little pencils and small boxes to write in. Happily, you can keep score with this app, which solves that little pet peeve. It's also nice to save your data, and see how your scores improve or deteriorate. To play a hole, simply select Play a Round and off you go. Start mapping your shots, and you will likely make better club choices, and may even find yourself on the green more often, with fewer strokes.

**GET NEW MAPS:** The first thing you should do with this app is to explore golf courses you have always wanted to play. Next, you should find the courses you do play and plan your strategy to shoot below par. With all the waypoints measured out, you can even plan which club to use where. If your courses are not mapped, you can ask the developer to add them. I had my local course added in less than a week.

# Best Business Apps

Your Android-based phone is both an elegant device that will provide hours of entertainment and a handy tool for personal and business productivity. Android-based phones give you the power to be **productive wherever you are**. Whether you're figuring out where to **entertain** a client or what sort of **budget** you have for your Travel and Entertainment activities, or whether you're **managing projects**, transferring spreadsheets, editing **documents**, or preparing a presentation, your Android-based phone has both the muscle and the intelligence to make quick work of the **job** at hand.

This chapter shows you how to turn your Android-based phone into the Swiss Army knife of **productivity**. When you download the right apps, your phone can help you manage your time, to-do lists, ideas, and work environment, and show off your amazing skill for juggling documents and schedules. Android has some distinct advantages over other phone platforms, and in the following pages we highlight some of the apps and features that provide this advantage.

# Best App for Note Taking

## AK Notepad

**Free**
**Version: 1.9.5**
**Snaptic**

AK Notepad gives you a great environment to write, share, and manage all your notes. It's a straightforward app that allows you to get up and running quickly and easily. The reminder feature alerts you of impending deadlines—it's like having a calendar built into your notes. Once you've written your note, you can send it to a friend or colleague via email or SMS, or stick it to your main screen for a desktop shortcut. AK Notepad also provides a nice search feature that allows you to find your note using either the tags or a simple search when your to-do list starts getting long.

**EASY ENTRY:** You enter notes with a simple click, and start typing by a simple touch on the screen. The default note has the look of a traditional yellow legal pad, but you can change the background color to have a different offset color if you prefer more contrast. Another nice feature is that if you enter a URL in your note, it becomes a live link automatically without having to type any HTML.

**ADD AND GO:** Once you start adding notes, you'll see that they are listed in order of the date you entered them. To change this, go to your settings and change the Sort Order to either Modified Time, Created Time, or Title. I prefer ordering by title, because I find it more useful to look things up by subject rather than when I started writing it or when I edited it. If you click and hold on a note, you will be prompted to View, Edit, Delete, Share, Stick-it, or Export to text file.

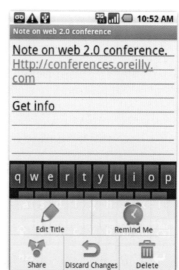

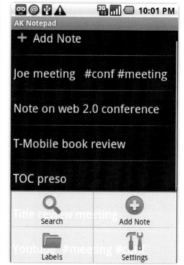

**Business**

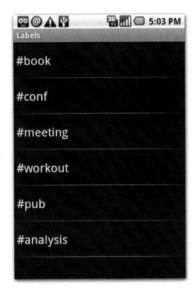

**HASHTAGS AS LABELS:** If you've ever used Twitter, you know that hashtags are a great way to tag content. A hashtag is simply a # sign followed by a word—for example, #projectX. AK Notepad allows you to use hashtags and access them later by browsing the Labels.

# Evernote
**Free**
**Version: 1.3**
**Evernote Corporation**

The notes that you take with the Evernote app can be accessed from both your Android device and your computer. You can quickly add a text note, audio note, photo snapshot, or file upload to your library from any of your devices. One particularly cool feature is Notes Nearby, which lets you find notes that were written near your current GPS location. I used this at a recent wine tasting event, and when I went back to the liquor store a few weeks later, I found my notes and exactly what I was looking for. Likewise, if you have a meeting in a particular conference room, you can use this feature to find your action items.

**QUICK VIEW:** You can view your notes using either the thumbnail view (the default) or as a list only. Evernote also allows you to sort your notes by date created or date updated, in ascending or descending order. Finding your items by search works well, too: just type in anything that may be in your note, and your results will be returned quickly. With this app you can take notes on your desktop machine and view them later on your phone or vice versa, so your notes are always there when you need them.

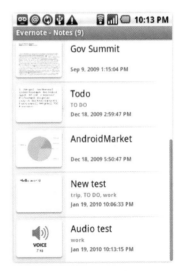

# Best App for Contact Management

## aContacts
**Free**
**Version: 1.3.3**
**Yermek Zhumagulov**

Most phones come with a decent standard address book for managing your contacts. However, the aContacts app takes contact management to another level by providing a picture-oriented interface, separate call settings for each contact, and multiple ways to connect to your contacts. One of the nice features of this app is how it takes advantage of Android's multitasking ability and "pops up" other apps to fulfill your requests. aContacts is a versatile way to store your contacts and access them quickly.

YOUR CONTACTS HAVE PERSONALITIES: Each of your contacts has a distinct personality, so that is precisely the way you should store them. If you have a mix of family, friends, and work contacts, why not group them or use similar ringtones for them so you know what type of call is coming in? aContacts provides plenty of customization control on each contact you store. You can even set call reminders so that you don't forget any scheduled calls.

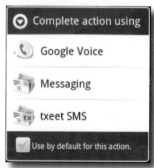

Business

TAKE NOTE: aContacts provides a laundry list of fields that you can use to store information about your contacts—for example, their social networks, job information, physical residence, instant messenger IDs, and personalized ringtones. Another nice feature is the call log, where you can see when you last spoke to or missed a call from your contact. The call log can be sorted by time, by contact, or by how long ago the call occurred.

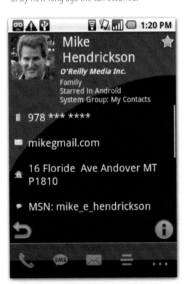

# Phonebook
**Free Lite version**
**Version: 1.0.6**
**Voxmobili SA / Online**

If you are looking for an app that's similar to the standard Contacts that comes with Android-based phones, you can't go wrong with Phonebook. It is oriented more toward phone contacts than social networks, so if you simply want to add your friends to a phonebook dialer, this is an excellent choice. In fact, I found this app so useful and intuitive that I created a shortcut and put it on my main screen to use as my phone dialer. There may be other apps that do more, but this one is simple, clean, and keeps your personal phonebook right at your fingertips.

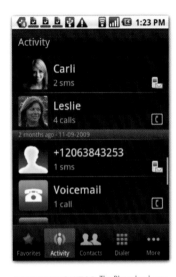

ACTIVITY MONITOR: The Phonebook app will display how you tend to interact with each contact. If you usually communicate via text, an SMS icon will appear next to that contact. If you get more calls, a call icon will appear. If you tap the name of a contact, it will bring up the history of your interaction, including SMS message threads and incoming and outgoing phone calls with dates. While in the activity section, you can also clear all data by selecting Menu and then Clear all logs.

39

# Best App for Accessing File Servers

## EStrongs File Explorer

**Free**
**Version: 1.0.4.0**
**EStrongs Inc.**

This is a powerful file explorer and manager that in my opinion is superior to most paid apps. It includes all the operations you need for file management, such as Copy, Cut, Paste, Delete, Rename, Select All, and Properties. It works directly with your operating system, letting you access your apps and kill, run, uninstall, back up, and even connect to LANs and FTP servers. You can hide any sensitive files that need protecting, and do file operations like editing text and zipping or unzipping files. You can even play audio and video locally or remotely.

**POWER GALORE:** If there's one word that describes this app, it's "Wow." If you have files on your work server, you can likely access them via the LAN tab by setting up and remembering a connection to a LAN server. This allows you to quickly authenticate and connect to your documents when they are stored on a server. Powerful stuff.

**ALL IN ONE:** This is the only app you need to manage files, directories, apps, services, and connections. From the Task Manager, you can click on the Applications tab and kill any apps that don't need to be running. Be careful, though, as some critical apps run in the background and take very few resources to do their job.

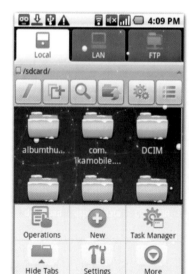

# Best App for Local File Browsing

## AndExplorer

**Free**
**Version: 1.3**
**Lysesoft**

When you need to quickly find a file on your device, this is a great app to have. You can explore the SD card or the device directories. You can also rename files, create directories, delete files, copy and paste files, and select your sort order. This allows you to browse your filesystems just as you would on your desktop computer. The AndExplorer app also provides Zip, Gzip, and Tar uncompressing capabilities for when someone sends you a packaged file or set of files.

**DEVICE BROWSING:** This app feels like Windows Explorer or the Finder on a Mac. It is easy to navigate by touching the item/folder you want to browse, or scrolling if you have a touch-ball on your device. There are options to Send, Refresh, Select all, Unselect all, and Clear Selection if you want to do mass activities like delete or copy.

**CUSTOM CHOICES:** You can set up your explorer to sort by any combination of file-name+size+date. You can also set your font to be more than 100% of the size you see on screen—nice for aging eyes. In addition, you can set the default encoding to UTF-8 or default (recommended).

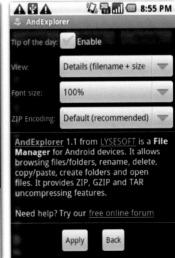

# Best File Server App

**Swi FTP**

## SwiFTP Server
Free
Version: 1.1.1
Dave Revell

Suppose you are traveling and want to share your files with colleagues but your company email is down. Fire up an FTP server and let your colleagues get whatever you designate for retrieval. Once you set this app up, you simply run the server and it will provide you with a server URL that can be shared with whomever you want accessing files. Whether you have music files, pictures, documents, or log files, you can make them easily accessible with this app.

**MINIMALIST DESIGN:** The design is exceedingly simple. Run and Stop are the two parameters you need to know, and enable the server log to see activity. Once the server is running, you can connect to it from a computer or device using the FTP client of your choice.

**SETTINGS SIMPLICITY:** The parameters you enter will be saved for future use, so next time you fire up the server all your settings will be remembered. You can share over WiFi or across the Net thanks to SwiFTP's global proxy.

Business

# Best File Transfer Client App

## AndFTP
Free
Version: 1.11
Lysesoft

This tool enables you to connect to FTP servers. It comes with both a device file browser and an FTP file browser, and provides download and upload features with resume support. You can use the device menu to rename, delete, copy, set permissions, and create folders. The AndFTP app provides support for FTP (File Transfer Protocol), SFTP (SSH's Secure File Transfer Protocol), and FTPS (Explicit FTP over TLS/SSL).

**TRANSFERRING LARGE FILES:** One of the perils of transferring large files to a mobile device is that the transfer will time out if you go out of range of the WiFi or cellular network. AndFTP allows you to securely transfer large files and resume if they time out during the transfer.

**A LITTLE MAINTENANCE:** You can also use this tool to clean up your directories. You can rename and delete files, create subdirectory folders, open and preview files, sort your files, and perform select all and unselect all functions. You can also use this tool to browse your handheld's files by clicking FTP file browser.

# Best App for Document Storage

## Teradesk Mobile

**Free**
**Version: 1.5**
**Teradesk e-Storage Systems**

Teradesk distinguishes itself through its flexibility, utility, and ease of use. Being a virtual file storage and remote file access tool, Teradesk uses secure encryption to transfer files to and from your Android device, and will automatically resume if your file transfer is interrupted. This app can process file transfers in the background while you work on something else. Teradesk can access your files that are on a server or device you point to, or that are up in the "cloud" of servers that Teradesk stores your virtual disk on.

**SMART FEATURES:** In addition to the standard folder types, you can add all sorts of other folders in which to store and access your content. This is a graphically rich UI that makes navigation easy and intuitive. Availability is not an issue, as the Teradisk is built on top of Amazon's cloud storage and server infrastructure. If you use the standard 1 gigabyte storage, you will not need to purchase more.

**SHARE IT, DON'T EMAIL IT:** With Teradesk you avoid using email to send files; instead, you can share your files with friends and coworkers with just one click. People can be notified via email or SMS about new documents and download files directly. It's easy to integrate Internet applications and Google Docs into your workflow. And instead of needing to bring your files to your local computer, you can just send them directly from cloud to cloud, using the large backbone of providers.

**CONTROL FILES:** File transfers are designed to resume transparently after connection problems. This resume feature really helps when you use mobile apps, and especially when transferring large files. In Android-based mobile phones, it is possible to have multiple file transfers occurring simultaneously. Teradesk give you lots of options on what to do with your files in the cloud. In short, this app never ceases to impress with its myriad options, features, and capabilities.

# SugarSync
**Free**
**Version: 1.5**
**Sharpcast, Inc.**

This app is not quite as full-featured as Teradesk, but it is very intuitive to set up and use. Its options and settings are minimal, and once you install the PC/Mac/Linux client you are able to share, protect, and access your files and directories on any designated computer that is connected to the Internet. One particularly handy feature is Share *<directoryname>*, which allows you to share your files with whomever you choose. Uploading files is pretty easy and if you use WiFi or 3G, it's fairly quick as well.

**AUTOMATIC TRANSFERS:** SugarSync uses local, remote, and cloud storage options. In short, you can access to your files on a computer and transfer them to your device or to a 2-gigabyte storage cloud provided by SugarSync. Edit any document directly on your phone, and SugarSync will detect the changes and automatically prompt you to upload the revisions to the cloud or your personal computer. The same holds true for taking photos: you will be prompted to save them to your cloud storage or personal computer.

45

# Best App for Mobile File Sharing

## GoAruna

**Free**
**Version: 1.2**
**Aruna Labs**

This is an intuitive yet full-featured app for storing and accessing files in Go-Aruna's "cloud" of storage servers. It provides many options for accessing files in GoAruna's storage servers or on your personal computer. The app allows you to perform actions on multiple files at once, which can be handy if you want to transfer several related files.

**LOCAL/REMOTE/CLOUD:** GoAruna offers a nice Desktop application that will show you what is on your local computer and on the cloud storage computer. Your Android device can see both places as well, and can get and put files in either space. The user interface is straightforward and easy to use, and there's a nice encryption feature that allows you to keep your documents safe and secure in the cloud or when transferring them around devices.

## DroidDrop

**Free**
**Version: 0.41**
**Carmen Delessio**

Quickly upload a file, put a password on it, and then annotate it, share it, or add links to it; DroidDrop has a number of options, but not so many that it complicates matters. You can repeat past drops, and set the expiration date of your drops.

46

# Best App for Peer-to-Peer File Sharing

## Transdroid

**Free**
**Version: 0.13.4**
**Eric Kok**

Use this app to transfer peer-to-peer Torrents. If you set up your desktop computer correctly, you can authenticate your phone and grab files that you have shared. You can also create log-ins for other folks and authorize them to grab copies of files on your phone. In this way, Transdroid is like a full-blown Torrent manager for your phone. This app can be set up to provide RSS feeds when new shares are found. It also has some nice filtering options, as well as the ability to set your transfer rates, both outgoing and incoming.

**SETUP:** Most of the work you have to do on this app is in the setup. In short, setup is not simple and is the only drawback to using this app. There is a great screencast at *http://vimeo.com/4537781* that shows you the basics. You can also make secure file transfers by setting up this app to access your desktop machine if you have a Torrent app installed there. The search feature is fast and simple, and with one click you can start your download.

| | 9:20 AM |
|---|---|
| **Search on-line for torrents** | |
| **O&apos;Reilly - 802.11 Wireless Networks - Definitive Guide [CuPpY]** 3.98585 MB | S: 0 L: 355 |
| **Rap | VA-Coast 2 Coast Instrumentals Vol 14(2009)** 107.005 MB | S: 109 L: 12 |
| **OReilly** 1188.37 MB | S: 60 L: 25 |
| **programming** 626.91 MB | S: 39 L: 17 |
| **OREILLY EBOOKS ISO** 550.18 MB | S: 44 L: 2 |
| OReilly | |

# Best Mobile Security App

Your phone's approximate location
2-128 Fawcett St, Cambridge, MA 02138, USA

Street View Available!
You can execute the commands below.
Alert I Lock I Backup I Wipe I Disconnect

## Mobile Defense
Free
Version: 1.2.3
Neevo, LLC

This app is great for those of use who have a tendency to lose our phones. Once installed, Mobile Defense allows you to remotely locate, lock, back up, or wipe your device, in addition to other neat features. One outstanding feature is that the app runs in the background and is undetected in your app list. So if a would-be thief takes your phone, he would not know you are tracking him, nor could he disable the app or uninstall it.

**STEALTH TRACKING:** Mobile Defense is very good at pinpointing a misplaced device. There is even a street view where you can highlight areas and zoom in. The map views are all viewable while the app is quietly running/sleeping in the background. The app wakes up only when it is asked to report on its whereabouts, so it is not a battery-drain.

**HIDDEN FEATURES** On the web page for your device, you can alert, lock, back up, wipe, or disconnect the device. The alert is a noisy siren, and it shrills loudly. The dashboard below shows the speed at which the device is moving, which is useful for determining how it is being transported and how quickly (by car, on foot).

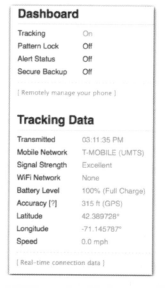

## Dashboard

| Tracking | On |
|---|---|
| Pattern Lock | Off |
| Alert Status | Off |
| Secure Backup | Off |

[ Remotely manage your phone ]

## Tracking Data

| Transmitted | 03:11:35 PM |
|---|---|
| Mobile Network | T-MOBILE (UMTS) |
| Signal Strength | Excellent |
| WiFi Network | None |
| Battery Level | 100% (Full Charge) |
| Accuracy [?] | 315 ft (GPS) |
| Latitude | 42.389728° |
| Longitude | -71.145787° |
| Speed | 0.0 mph |

[ Real-time connection data ]

48

Mobile Defense    HOME

| | 359444021181455's Activity | Recent Locations | Phone Details |

**Phone Details**

| | |
|---|---|
| Status | Active |
| Device ID (IMEI / MEID) | 359444021181455 |
| Build Brand | T-mobile |
| Build Model | T-mobile mytouch 3g |
| Phone Type | GSM |
| Operating System | Android 1.6 |
| Mobile Defense Version | 1.2.3 |
| Current Line Number | (206) |
| Last Updated | 01-09-2010 08:17PM |

**Current SIM Details**

| | |
|---|---|
| Status | Active |
| Mobile Operator | T-Mobile |
| Serial Number | 8901260250035981114 |
| Subscriber ID | 310260253598111 |
| Line Number | (206) |
| Country | US |

**WEB INTERFACE:** Mobile Defense has some nifty tools that help you recover your phone. You'll see all the locations where your phone has been traveling as well as any changes in the SIM card. The would-be thief may look to see what apps are running by checking Manage Applications in your phone settings. However, Mobile Defense will remain hidden, since it's usually dormant and only awakens to take a reading of your device's location. Unfortunately, the app also sends an SMS message that alerts you of the activity, which could be a tip-off to a would-be thief. For workarounds, check the FAQ on the Mobile Defense website.

# Mobile Security
**Free**
**Version: Beta 4.4.2**
**Lookout**

If you are moving attachments around, you should be concerned about viruses, damage, and theft/loss of your phone. Mobile Security, formerly Flexilis, offers protection against all three in an intuitive app. When installed, the app runs in the background, so a would-be thief will not be aware of its presence. This and other security apps could also be used track a person's whereabouts, if you were so inclined.

**GOT A BACKUP PLAN:** We've all seen it happen: you lose your phone, or it gets run over by a street paver, or dropped in water and everything is toast. Using the Data Backup feature in Mobile Security provides you with a secure copy of all your data files (contacts, pictures, etc.) on the Web, where you can restore the data quickly and easily.

# Best App for Secure Money Transfers

## PayPal

**Free**
**Version: 1.1.1**
**eBay**

There's nothing revolutionary here, but for regular PayPal users this will be a welcome addition to their Android-based phone. If you have a PayPal account, you could theoretically get your paychecks via PayPal, have a PayPal debit MasterCard, and pretty much do away with a traditional bank account. Wouldn't it be nice not to worry about carrying money around? PayPal also integrates with your contact list and allows you to transfer money to anyone, whether or not you know their email address or account numbers.

**BALANCE YOUR CHECKBOOK:** Your recent history allows you to see all the transactions during the previous couple of months, so you can determine whether a payment has cleared, been processed, or is still outstanding. You'll also see a handy balance history page.

**DIGITAL GREEN:** PayPal is the leader in providing Internet payments to all sorts of commerce sites. Mobile payments are kept safe using the same technology that PayPal uses to secure web-based transactions.

**PayPal**

Send money

Carli Hendrickson

30.00    USD

Lunch Money

| Cancel | Continue |

Balance | History | Send Money | Info

**PayPal**

**PayPal Mobile info**

PayPal Mobile lets you review your PayPal account balance, send and receive money, shop, or make donations by text message or mobile web on your mobile phone.

Sign up

To sign up for PayPal Mobile, go to www.paypal.com/mobile

Conctact us

For more information about PayPal Mobile, go to www.paypal.com/mobile or call 1-888-221-1161

Forgot password?

To recover a forgotten password, go to www.paypal.com/forgotpassword

PIN log in

Add a mobile phone PIN to your PayPal account and log in fast - there's no need to enter your email address or password. To create a pin go to m.paypal.com

Balance | History | Send Money | Info | Log out

# App for Purchasing Goods

## Amazon.com
**Free**
**Version: 1.0.1**
Amazon.com

Sure, you could just use your browser to go to Amazon, but why? This app stores all the useful stuff for you in one click, without having to type all that http stuff. This is a very cool app, and if you believe that apps could one day replace websites, be sure to check it out. There is no reason to use the browser for Amazon shopping when you have an app like this. It remembers the settings that you have on the Web and clones them for your device. (There are a whole bunch of Amazon apps, so make sure you get the one made by "Amazon.com.")

**YOU KNOW WHAT YOU WANT:** And with this app, you can go get it. If you *don't* know exactly what you want, Amazon will have recommendations for you based on your purchasing history. One particularly cool feature that is found only on this app is the ability to take a picture, or scan a barcode, and have Amazon find you the product or save it with your account until something similar shows up.

**SEARCH AWAY:** I often use Amazon to get more information about a product, and to Amazon's credit, this search often converts to a sale. With search on your device, Amazon has that same great shopping experience. It feels like your device knows your preferences, what you look at, and what you purchase. More often than not, my research turns into purchases because the app brings back relevant items, including ones I didn't know I wanted.

# Best App for Money Management

## EasyMoney

Free
Version: 1.2.2
Handy Apps

This app is a versatile money manager that tracks expenses and has reminders built in for a variety of things. Other useful features include bill-pay reminders, multiple accounts and currencies, fully customizable income/expense categories, transfers between accounts, budgets, and reports. This app has many predefined budget categories and includes a New Category feature, so you can customize your budget and get your expenses well organized.

**QUICK VIEW OF ACCOUNTS:** The Accounts Overview button takes you to a dashboard that shows you all the accounts you have and their current balances. If you drill down on an account, you will see all transactions and transfers into and out of the account during a chosen period of time. You can also add a recurring transaction to the account directly through this screen.

**CHECK OUT YOUR HISTORY:** The reports menu offers all sorts of graphical reports that allow you to view your money and transactions in a variety of ways, including custom time periods and filtered by categories. The cash flow report is awesome for showing you what is going on monthly with your deposits and withdrawals.

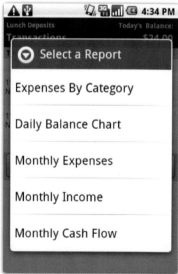

Barnes & Noble Booksellers #2806
906 Mall Loop Road
High Point, NC 27262
336-886-1331

STR:2806 REG:007 TRN:6567 CSHR:Eric H

Best Android Apps
9781449382551          T1
(1 @ 19.99)                        19.99

                                   19.99
Subtotal                            1.55
Sales Tax T1 (7.750%)
TOTAL                              21.54
VISA                               21.54
  Card#: XXXXXXXXXXXX2443
  Expdate: XX/XX
  Auth:   145628
  Entry Method: Swiped

A MEMBER WOULD HAVE SAVED            2.00

Thanks for shopping at
Barnes & Noble

101.23B                12/14/2010  06:52PM

CUSTOMER COPY

**DGET LIKE A PRO:** If you just want to track
bers, there are plenty of apps that can do
However, if you want to put together a real
et with complete reporting and account
action detail, this is the app for you. You can
t a PIN authentication on this app to keep
ensitive information private.

**MULTIPLE ACCOUNT TYPES:** If you want to
track your Visa, Amex, MasterCard, or other credit
card, there are 10 built-in account types that you
can select from. In this way, you can manage all
your finances, from trivial payments to large
mortgages and assets. You can even apply filters
to all your transactions.

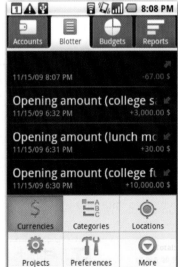

# Best App for Personal Finance

## FireWallet
**Free 30-day Trial / $6.99 Full version**
**Version: 3.0.0**
**James Gramata**

This app is another great way to manage your finances. It is ideal for when you are traveling and need to separate your personal expenditures from your business expenses. Another nice feature lets you keep an eye on your finances while you are on the go. You can transfer funds between accounts and view your transaction history. You can also add, copy, edit, view, sort, purge, and export and import transactions.

**ACCOUNT MANAGEMENT:** Account management with this app is simple, and there are many options for managing your accounts. You can specify whether the account balance can be negative, the type of account (six choices), and whether the account balance should be included in your total balance. There's space for notes and websites so you can enter more information about each account.

**TRANSACTION MANAGEMENT:** Once you have set up your accounts, you can add debit and credit transactions. Particularly helpful is the recurrence feature, which allows you to have recurring debits (bills) and credits (paychecks). You can also specify whether or not a particular transaction was in one of your budgets, which helps track unbudgeted expenditures.

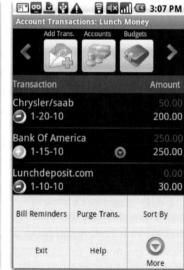

# NeatPayment

**Free Lite / $2.99 Full version**
**Version: 1.3**
**Prolog Inc.**

As its name implies, this app really is neat. Whether you're selling or buying, this makes credit card payments easier and faster. It currently works on two major online payment gateways: Authorize.Net and PayPal Payflow Pro. With NeatPayment, you can pay or accept payment even if you don't have a credit card terminal, and better yet, it imposes no additional cost per transaction. This is a handy way to buy or sell when you are on the road or at a trade show or convention.

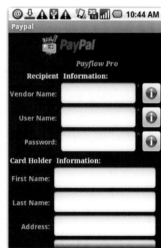

**NEATO:** You can get paid by credit card, no matter how small your business. NeatPayment allows you to check funds and then authorize the major credit card types for any transaction you have. Using Authorize.Net as one of your payment options, you can even complete a credit card transaction to sell your old sneakers at a yard sale.

**PAYPAL INTERFACE:** Even if your potential customer doesn't have a credit card, you can still do business with them by using PayPal. Since PayPal is a trusted service, you get all of its built-in protections, whether you are selling or buying.

# Best App for Scanning Prices/Goods

## Barcode Scanner
**Free**
**Version: 3.0.1**
**ZXing Team**

This is a simple but powerful app. Just scan a barcode, and the Barcode Scanner app will fetch information about the product, including how to purchase the item. You can decode one-dimensional barcodes like the ones found on books, or QR Codes like you find on the Web and in print. You can use this app to access Google Book Search and navigate to the book content. This app also allows you to search other product codes.

**BOOKWORMS TAKE NOTE:** Be sure that there's sufficient lighting when you make your scan. I also found that after you scan one product, you may need to exit the app and relaunch it before you scan a second product. Another limitation I found is that it is difficult to scan products on irregular surfaces, so I tend to restrict my usage of this app to books, where it excels.

**QUICK SEARCH:** Google Book Search also lets you quickly search inside the book. You'll be prompted for a string to find, and then you're off to the races. The Barcode Scanner allows you to navigate directly to a book on Google Book Search (*books.google.com*) and find reviews, descriptions, and more. If you install this app, try it out on our QR Code index (page 226).

# Best App for Comparing Items

## Compare Everywhere

**Free**
**Version: 1.3**
**Compare Everywhere**

The Compare Everywhere app uses the Open Source barcode scanning techniques developed by ZXing. All you need to do is scan an item's barcode, and the app returns a list of comparison prices and reviews if they are available. You can modify the search radius, but by default the results will consist of stores within 20 miles. Another nice feature of this app is the ability to create a list of items you have compared; you can then export the list to HTML or XML.

**SCANNING POINTS:** Scanning a product using this app is much like what happens at a grocery store or pharmacy, but here the scan uses the camera function to take a picture once the barcode is recognized. The information on books is very good, but other items will often return "item not found" results.

**MAP TO YOUR PRODUCT SEARCH:** Because your phone knows exactly where you are, it can give directions to the closest places to purchase your compared item. Sometimes convenience and immediacy are more important than getting the cheapest price.

# Best App for Stock Market Tracking

## Quote Pro
**Free**
**Version: 1.2**
**Quirk Consulting, Inc.**

Quote Pro is a great app that boasts a number of useful features, including numbered profiles. You can list a few stocks you want to track in one portfolio, and then with a tap of a finger you can see your other portfolios. This is useful when tracking different sectors of the market, and allows for comparisons based on the stocks you want to group. Quotes are provided by Yahoo! and include the major indices. There is a 20-minute time delay, but Quote Pro refreshes prices every 10 seconds.

**TRACKING:** Start with just a few stocks, and add however many you want. Adding a stock is simple—as you type on the keyboard, stock symbols begin to auto fill and you can select from the choices. The Options menu allows you to define sort orders, colors, refresh rates, and the level of detail you want displayed for each stock.

**DRILL DOWN:** Press the menu button to view the options of News, Chart, Details, Delete, and Cancel. The Details option provides high and low trends along with a handy chart; click it to find more information online. The Chart selection offers a whole set of charting options, including comparisons, time ranges, line types, chart types, and the ability to define two subcharts.

# Android Finance

Free
Version: 2.0
Google

You can use this app to view stock performance over one day, five days, one month, six months, one year, five years, or the maximum time available. Only one portfolio is allowed (even though the label indicates "Portfolios"). The app has decent charting of the major indices and does a good job charting the stocks in your portfolio. The News tab takes you to all the Google news relating to the symbol or index you click on. Set the default view to be *max to date*, and you can view trends.

# Stocks

Free
Version: 0.4.0
Dato

This is another simple tool that allows you to view the performance of stocks and major indices over one day, one month, or one year. It is simple to add a stock to watch, and you can add as many as you want, though you'll have to scroll to see their performance. There is no portfolio feature in this app, but you can organize your stocks however you like. Place the indices at the top and order stocks alphabetically to keep things manageable. This is an installable app, not the one that comes installed on some phones.

**SIMPLE CHARTING:** The charting feature in the Stocks app is a tiny graph that offers multiple options. You can modify the date range; add, delete, or rename symbols; and move symbols up, down, and to the top or bottom of the list. The main settings allow you to choose your color scheme, and whether you want to see percent, price, or both.

# Best App for Being a Local

## ALOQA

**Free**
**Version: 1.4.1**
**Aloqa GmbH**

Wherever you go, ALOQA lets you "Always Be a Local." In this app, you set the channels you want to follow and the app proactively pushes content your way based on your location. Use this app to find out what's available and what's going on nearby. The app also integrates map-level views of the pushed content, making it easy to find things even if you're a stranger in a strange land.

**CHANNEL YOUR ACTIVITIES:** There are more than 30 channels to subscribe to, bringing you content from a variety of major categories such as Auto, Fast Food, Coffee, Hospitals, Movies, Pizza, and others. You can also set your notification style for each channel: an alarm, a vibration, or just a number displayed. This is a handy app that can be tailored to your preferences in entertainment, food, and so on.

**FIND YOUR CHANNEL:** One nice feature lets you go directly from content that is pushed to you through a channel to driving directions to the event, activity, or establishment. Start with your current location and let ALOQA and your GPS find your destination with either normal, satellite, or traffic map modes. All the normal Google Maps features apply once you begin your journey to a local destination.

Business

# Best App for Finding Activities

## Sherpa

**$2.99**
**Version: 1.1.10**
**Geodelic Systems, Inc.**

The Sherpa app tailors itself to your preferences. If you are entertaining prospective business partners, Sherpa uses Web2.0-style profiling with location-based and contextual data to suggest nearby attractions, restaurants, and retailers. If you eat out more than you shop, the app shows more restaurants than retail stores. In addition, Sherpa only gives suggestions that are pertinent to the time of day, so if you run a search at 2:00 a.m. looking for government offices, you won't get much.

**YOU KNOW WHAT YOU WANT:** But you are in the middle of nowhere. Upon startup, Sherpa gives you a quick view of the nearby establishments in a scrolling list called Carousel view. This can be switched to either a map view or a simple list view. The results can then be narrowed down by type, such as groceries, dining, banks, movie theaters, cafes and coffeeshops, nightclubs and bars, arts and culture, and so forth.

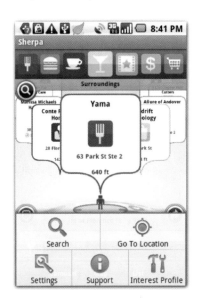

 HONORABLE MENTION

## Where

**Free**
**Version: 1.8.5**
**where**

This location-based app helps you connect to places and people. I particularly like the red-dot feature that pinpoints and aggregates what people in the vicinity are saying on social media.

# Best App for Finding Restaurants

## Zagat To Go '10

**$9.99**
**Version: 1.1**
**Handmark**

If you want to impress a potential business partner, of course you'll use the most trusted guide to restaurants. Zagat To Go is a great app, and if you are familiar with using Zagat guides for selecting a restaurant, you'll love this. It uses your GPS location to bring back the most relevant spots to where you are at the moment. The options allow you to use your current location, a particular city or region, an exact address, or to select from your recent locations. You also select the radius you want to search within.

**CONTEXT ORIENTED:** If you travel 3,000 miles to meet a client, do you want to spend time looking for a suitable restaurant or would you rather trust Zagat's to steer you? Sure, you could ask a concierge, but this app is convenient and customizable. If you know Zagat's and trust them, you can't go wrong here.

**DECIDE WHAT YOU WANT:** One of the best features of this app is that it can tell you what's in the neighborhood or give you results by cuisine type, or you can get results based on other features such as Children Friendly, Delivery, Live Entertainment, Romantic, Singles Scene, and a host of other options. I've learned more about the restaurants in my area through this app than I have eating at them for the past 10 years.

# Best App for Dining Reservations

## OpenTable

Free
Version: 1.0.8
OpenTable, Inc.

OpenTable helps you make reservations at local dining establishments. This app provides links to menus, reviews, location, and most importantly seat availability at local restaurants. You'll never again walk up to the latest trendy restaurant only to be turned away because there are no seats left. If you do use this app and discover that a restaurant has no spots left, it doesn't hurt to call them—there are often cancellations.

LET YOUR FINGERS DO THE WALKING: There are more than 100 metro areas found in OpenTable, and you can decide whether you want to stay in the city or reach out into the suburbs. Staying metro will search all the metro restaurants of your choice. It's also useful to indicate party size, particularly when you have a large party and want to ensure you can be accommodated.

RESERVE YOUR TABLE: Before you go to any restaurant, you can find out what times are available and learn about the restaurant. The number of $ signs indicates how pricey the establishment is. When you click on a time, you'll be prompted to enter your reservation details.

# Best App for Sharing Favorite Places

## UrbanKite

Free
Version: 1.0.8
UrbanKite

This app lets you discover local establishments and activities. Once you find something, you'll see the address and how far away you are—results are sorted by distance, from closest to farthest away. Whether you need to get a haircut, catch a bus, or virtually anything else, this app will give you the relevant results with all the details you need. After you've found the establishment you are looking for, use this app to share your thoughts about it.

**ALL WALKS OF LIFE:** There are as many categories in UrbanKite as there are in Google Local. With this app, you can pinpoint your area of interest, and once your genre is displayed, click on an establishment and you will be taken to a detail page where you can call or map your destination. Click "Details on Google" and you will get full details, reviews, and anything else that is found on Google. Very nice.

**SHARE YOUR COOL SPOTS WITH OTHERS:** One of the really cool features of this app is its integration with Twitter. Once you enter your Twitter login credentials, you can comment, share, and rate your destination all via Twitter and UrbanKite. So don't just grab a cup at Starbucks—let others know you are there and join a few friends.

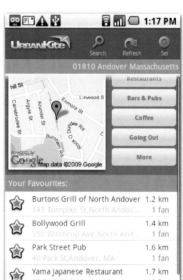

Business

**SEARCH FOR YOUR INTEREST:** Discover local establishments and activities, including restaurants, pubs and bars, coffeeshops, bistros, nightclubs, transportation locations, arts and culture, banks, sporting, medical centers, sightseeing, government offices, and much more.

# Places Directory

**Free**
**Version: 1.0.17**
**Google Places Directory Team**

This is a simple location-aware app that provides basic local categories for you to browse through. These 13 categories should cover just about anything you might need. This app does not learn your tendencies like Sherpa does, but is useful and intuitive for your everyday needs. There is no setup and very little to do other than tap away on the screen. You can customize this app by setting your distance to metrics or feet, and you can clear the history to cover your tracks. This simple app can be a real time-saver and helper.

**DESIGN SIMPLICITY:** This is an easy app to use. There are no channels, preferences, or anything else to set. Just fire it up and it figures out where you are and what is close by. You can read available reviews, view pictures in the gallery, and see where the item is found on a map.

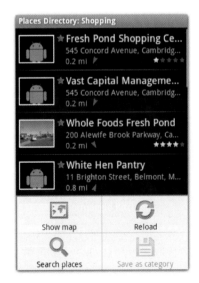

# Best PDF App

## Scan2PDF Mobile

**£3.99**
**Version: 2.0.4**
**Burrotech**

Scan2PDF Mobile is a simple-to-use app that does just what you think it does. Hover your phone over the document you want to "scan" and click the Scan Page button. This takes a picture of the document. Make sure it's readable, and then press the Make PDF button to turn it into a PDF file. The "delete page" and "delete all" options can be used to re-scan a page if it didn't turn out correctly, or to delete all of the scanned pages for your document before you turn it into a PDF file. Use the options in the menu key to specify the scan quality, auto-rotate, and options for making the PDF (size, output folder, filenames, and more).

**SMART FEATURES:** You can build multi-page documents by scanning pages one after another. Scan2PDF remembers how many pages it has, and when you press Make PDF it will save them all into one file. If you need a high-quality scan, you can set the level to Ultra for large but clear documents. The rotate page view can be helpful when previewing your pages, so you don't have to cram a horizontal page into a vertical view.

**EMAIL YOUR DOCUMENT:** Once all your pages are set and you click on Make PDF, you will see the dialog box below. This gives you the option to email the file, view it, or delete the pages after the PDF has been created. Deleting the pages helps maintain a clean filesystem by getting rid of old documents.

Business

**OPTIONS:** Make sure to set default behaviors for all the PDFs you create. Select a size, a directory on your SD card, and an output name. I have given all my PDFs the prefix *mob_* so I know it's from my mobile device. I save the files to a directory on my desktop, and then I can search for *mob_* to find a PDF I made on the run.

 **HONORABLE MENTION**

# BeamReader
**Free**
**Version: 0.99.4**
**SLG Mobile, Inc.**

This app lets you view and zoom in on your PDF documents. There is very little configuration or setup, and it's very intuitive to use—after all, you're just viewing a PDF. So if someone sends you a PDF or you came across one while browsing the Web on your device, this free tool will let you easily see what you want. You can even view the PDF as plain text if you open the menu and toggle Text View.

**QUICK VIEW:** Fire up this app and your PDF document is ready to view. When you have multipage PDF files, you can click on the menu key and launch a search by page number or keyword find. In this way you can save yourself the trouble of scrolling, which is very handy for longish PDFs. You also have the option to save the file to your SD card, which is useful when someone sends you an email with a PDF file attached.

# Best App for Tracking Packages

## Package Tracking
Free
Version: 1.0.2
Technogeek00

Who knew that tracking your precious cargo using your phone could be even easier than tracking it on the Web? This slick little app tracks packages from more than 10 delivery services and maps your package's current location. Another interesting feature is the ability to scan the barcode on your package and track it that way. Or you can input an old tracking number and get information on a previous delivery.

**AUTO REMEMBER:** If you send and receive lots of packages, this app is for you. In the settings, you can auto-save numbers so you don't have to keep entering the number over and over again. You can also have the app bring up your last-used number, which is helpful when you're tracking a specific package. After all, why retype all those numbers when you don't have to?

**MISTER SCANMAN:** The barcode scanner in this app works wonderfully—in face, the camera seems to work better here than it does in the Barcode Scanner app. You can scan package after package without having to restart. This app also stores your package information, so you can go back and check or delete the status.

# Mobile Package Tracker

$0.99
Version: 1.3.0
Minstech

This is a good alternative for tracking shipped packages. You can set up notifications to alert you of status changes in your package's journey. This app allows you to perform three simple actions: tracking your package, getting a list of all your packages, and getting information on each shipment. You can enable notifications, set the types of alerts and frequency of updates, track the status level (out for delivery or all changes in status), and more.

**THE TRACKER:** Tracking packages is pretty straightforward—you don't even need to be on the Web. Simply type your tracking number into the app or scan your label before you send it out the door. The main consumer-oriented shippers are your default choices—FedEx, UPS, DHL, USPS, and TNT. You can enable the shippers you use and disable the ones you have no interest in using.

**THE PACKAGE:** The package interface in this app is simple. Any numbers you have entered or barcodes you have scanned are saved in the Packages tab. This makes it much easier to keep track of things if you have a few packages going at once. From here you can either track the package, edit its details, or remove it from your tracking history. I find that this is the tab I use most when tracking my packages.

# Best Communication Apps

Your Android-based phone is a great business tool, entertainment device, lifestyle companion, and travel aid, and it has many other uses as well. One of its most basic and important functions is to communicate. Nowadays, communication refers to many different things, including **broadcasting**, **tweeting**, **podcasting**, **emailing**, **texting**, and myriad other forms of connecting with someone or something else. Android-powered phones excel at connecting people, devices, and applications, and thus enable more effective communication.

In this chapter we discuss a few Android apps that center around communication, connections, and transmitting a message, file, or something else from one place to another. The Android market is full of communication apps, but we will highlight only those we feel are most useful and that have been rated the highest.

So whether you're looking for a great **texting** app or a better way to **sync your email** with your phone, you'll want to spend some quality time with this chapter.

# Best SMS App

## chompSMS
Free
Version: 2.18
chompSMS

All Android-powered phones come with built-in messaging apps, but for an excellent texting environment you can't beat chompSMS. It has a clean interface and it's loaded with many other nice features and options. The Settings menu lets you customize the app to your style of texting, and you can create shortcuts for your most frequently used character sequences. Generally, SMS messaging allows you to send 160 characters (unless you switch to Unicode, which has a maximum of 70 characters).

**SMART FEATURES:** The chompSMS text window is in the familiar bubble style, and you can set the bubbles to be color coded. The top of the dialog window shows who you are texting with, and at the bottom you'll see how many messages you have sent to this person. The character and SMS counter make clear how many characters remain for the text being entered.

**OPTIMIZE YOUR $ FOR TEXT:** Among all the great features for chompSMS, there are even some options that help save you money when sending messages. The Quick Switch feature lets you easily choose between sending messages over the chompSMS network and using your mobile carrier. This comes in handy when roaming internationally, as you can avoid the extra charges for sending and receiving messages.

Communication

# Another Best SMS App

## Handcent SMS

Free
Version: 2.9.28
Handcent Software

Handcent is another powerful SMS app for you to consider. With more than 40 options in the Settings menu, you can tune this app's environment to exactly what you want. The batch mode allows you to select a bunch of messages at once and delete them, and there's a quick button to call the person you are texting if you are so inclined. You can also set distinct notifications and styles of text formatting for each contact. For example, you could use this to distinguish between personal contacts and work contacts.

**EASY INTERFACE:** If you just want to send a quick text with something like "What are you up to," you can select one of nine preloaded messages. While you are composing a text message, you can click the menu to attach media, files, or other items that you want delivered to your recipient. You also have the option to insert 17 different smiley faces, if you like that sort of thing. There's even an explanation next to each set of text symbols. It's pretty B-).

**TIRED OF TYPING ON A SMALL SCREEN?:** This app lets you speak text messages and then translates them to text that you can edit or send as is. The translation of the voice data is decent, but not perfect. Like most voice-recognition apps, you really need to articulate clearly, speak loudly, and go slowly. It's a fun feature to play around with. I "speak text" with my daughter and we try to figure out what the other said. Not the intended purpose, but entertaining nonetheless.

# Other Apps for Text Messaging

**HONORABLE** MENTION

### txeet: SMS Templates
Free
Version: 1.0.4
Just2us

If style is important to you, you'll definitely want to check out the txeet app. It offers a bunch of templates to style your messages, including Accented Latin, RAnDoM CaPs, Scmabrle Eggs, and Vwl Removal. The templates fall into six major categories, organized around standard themes. You can also insert traditional emoticons, as well as some hip new ones. And thank goodness for the Lingo feature, which allows me to decipher what my teenage daughters send me.

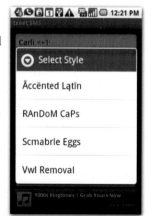

**HONORABLE** MENTION

### Unavailable
$1
Version: 1.2.3
alienmanfc6

If you are too busy to answer repeated text messages, just set your auto-reply message with this app. You can define a list of people who get auto-replies, and have custom replies sent automatically. This can be a big help in dealing with marketing groups or people who continuously send you messages instead of a longer email. You can also set this app to kick in after certain hours when you do not want to be interrupted with text messages, but you still want your phone on for calls. Or you can simply have the app send an away message to anyone who texts you.

# Best App for Finding WiFi

## WiFi Buddy
Free
Version: 0.9.1-Beta
André Rabold

WiFi Buddy lets you combine your device settings, wireless controls, and WiFi settings in one click. The preferences for this app make it particularly useful. You choose when to switch from WiFi to mobile, when to scan for new networks, and what your device should do based on your location. It also has some nice security features that allow you to password-protect the encryption keys you've saved for various wireless networks. When you want a network connection, searching and connecting is only one click away with this handy app.

## WiFinder
Free
Version: 1.4
pgmsoft

WiFinder is a fast and easy-to-use app that connects your device to a WiFi network. It's a lot simpler than diving into your wireless settings and then selecting, forgetting, and so on. The visual display mode shows how strong your connection is, and you can choose to view it as a percentage or in dBm (power ratio). Leaving auto-scan on will help you locate WiFi, but will also wear down your battery. I'd turn it on only when you need it.

# Best Instant Messaging App

## eBuddy

Free
Version: 1.5.0
eBuddy

If you prefer instant messaging to texting, or if you need to communicate with people in your office who use IM, this app is ideal for you. It connects you to all your IM accounts and brings them together in one window. The menu button quickly brings you to the Add Buddy and Settings screens, and the three tabs at the top quickly take you to your list of buddies, the chats you have going, and the accounts you have set up.

**SEE WHO'S ONLINE:** eBuddy lets you see who is online and who is away, without having to log into all of your different networks. It is very easy to add more buddies through the drop-down window that shows a list of the networks you have an account on.

**MULTIPLE CHAT PLATFORMS, NO PROBLEM:** If you're like most people, you have instant messenger friends on AIM, MSN, Yahoo!, Facebook, GoogleTalk, ICQ, MySpace, and various other places. eBuddy lets you pull all of these different services into one window. You'll like not having to switch back and forth or install separate apps for each account. Just one eBuddy account gets everybody together on one screen.

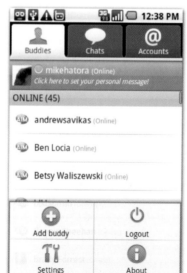

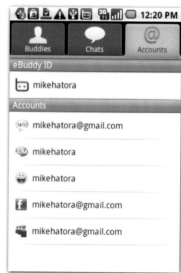

Communication

**SET YOUR AVAILABILITY:** One great feature of eBuddy is that you can set your status to "appear offline," so potential time-interrupters are thwarted before they can bother you. This can be particularly useful if you are buried in a project because you can leave your phone on for emergency calls but not have to deal with the interruptions of constant IMing. You can set your availability as Busy, Online, Away, or Appear Offline; you can also provide a custom status, like "At the Dentist" or whatever works at the moment.

 **HONORABLE MENTION**

# Palringo
**Free**
**Version: 1.0b4**
**Palringo Limited**

This is a strong honorable mention, as Palringo is an instant messaging client specifically designed for mobile, making it really simple to use. Chat and send picture and voice messages to all your friends from one contact list. Taking advantage of Android's multitasking abilities, you can keep in touch with all your buddies on the most popular IM services without installing or switching between different applications. Palringo allows you to chat to your friends on MSN, AIM, iChat, ICQ, Yahoo!, Jabber, Gtalk, Gadu-Gadu, and Facebook.

**SENDING PICS:** One nice feature of this messaging app is that you can also send pictures or images. If you press the picture icon, you'll be prompted to take a photo with your phone's camera. So when you are climbing Mt. Everest, snap some shots and send them to whomever you have in your address book. You can also send an image that you've already saved to your device.

# Best Twitter App

## Twidroid
**Free / €3.99 Pro version**
**Version: 3.0.9**
**Zimmermann & Marban**

If you use Twitter, get this app and you'll be sure not to miss any of the action. There are as many features loaded into this app as you would get in a desktop client. When you compose a tweet, you have the option to insert a photo or video, record video, or take a photo that you can attach to your tweet. You can also manage and view tweets for multiple accounts. Clicking on a tweet will pop up the options to Reply, Show Profile, Favorite, Retweet, Send DM, Copy to Clipboard, Share Tweet, and Report Spam. Share Tweet lets you send it to other social networks, email, and texting apps.

**HIT THE ROAD @JACK:** Twidroid allows you to hit the road and not miss a tweet. You can choose to display between 50 and 250 tweets at a time using the five preset select buttons. I've configured Twidroid to display 180 tweets at a time, and often use the Jump to Top button to return to the top of the list when the newest messages filter in.

**PRACTICAL STEPS:** Even the free version of Twidroid offers some powerful features in the Settings tab. You can select which photo and video services to use, the quality of the images, your preferred URL shortener service, the Geolocation data that is transmitted with your tweets, and other sweet goodies. And the Pro version unlocks even more features.

Communication

# Seesmic

**Free**
Version: 1.1
Seesmic

Don't let the honorable mention fool you—this app is neck-and-neck with Twidroid. The free Seesmic has many of the same features as the Pro version of Twidroid, though with less options to select from. If you use the desktop or web version of Seesmic, you'll love this app. It's clean and very intuitive to use, and packs a whole lot of features into a tiny little app. You can use your Bit.ly username and API key, making it easy to track your tweeted short URLs and resulting clicks. You can also set all sorts of notifications to alert you of various updates and messages.

**SAVE YOUR POWER:** You can help save your battery by adjusting the interval to check for new messages from every five minutes to once every hour. If you limit the number of tweets you pull in on each poll, that will help even more. Using the five preset selections, you can set the app to fetch between 20 and 150 tweets on each update. So if you set your updates to be once an hour and grab 150 tweets at a time, you'll save your battery but may miss a few tweets. You can always manually refresh to get new tweets.

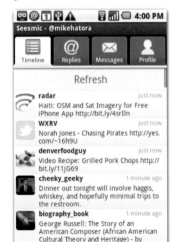

# Twitta

**Free**
Version: 10
DART

Twitta is a basic Twitter client with clean, simple menus and few settings. If you are new to Twitter, you may want to start with this app before moving up to the more full-featured apps previously mentioned. The one advanced feature is that you can set the application to check for new tweets even when the app is not running. Turning this feature on will eat your battery, however, so keep that in mind when setting the update interval.

# Best App for Sending Email

## K-9 Mail
Free
Version: 2.109
K-9 Dog Walkers

K-9 Mail is an excellent free and open source email client that can handle IMAP, POP, WebDav, and some not-so-finicky exchange servers. This app is an improved and more full-featured version of the Mail app that comes with your Android phone. You have control over how often you poll for messages and the number of messages to display. Even if your phone is not your primary email client, you may want to use a client like this to check mail when you are between places.

**21 SETTINGS:** K-9 Mail provides many, many options to set your email environment just the way you want it. If you have folders stored on your server and filters to direct mail into those different folders, you can elect to check these folders or not. For instance, I set up a folder into which I filter any message that has an attachment and is not from my company's domain. I don't check this folder with K-9—those messages can wait until I get to the office.

**QUICK ACTIONS:** Once you open an email, you can take quick action on the message using the menu button. Your standard Reply, Reply All, Forward, Mark Unread, and Delete are all just a click away. This makes handling your email easy and fast. I can browse my email and scan for spam, then quickly nuke it. This way, when I get to my office I have few spam mails left, and less work to get to the heart of my inbox.

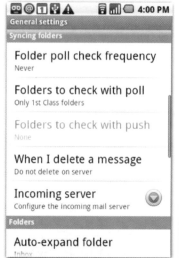

# SMS Email

**Free**
**Version: 0.1.9**
**Peter Baldwin**

Want to send email without using a data plan? SMS Email is a bare-bones app that lets you send text messages to email addresses. This is a great solution if you ever find yourself without a WiFi connection and do not have (or do not want to use) a data plan. The setup is simple: you just select from 20 carrier plans or a custom setup. One nice feature is the autocomplete when entering a name; you can also select from your address book.

**ROAMING AROUND:** If you are traveling to some remote place and have cell reception but not data, you can use this app to send email. For example, on a recent visit to the U.S. Virgin Islands, I selected USA / T-Mobile in the settings menu. Data roaming charges would have been expensive, so I used the SMS Email app to send a couple of emails to friends and family.

# Voice On The Go

**Free 15-day trial**
**Version: 0.9.3**
**Voice on the Go Inc.**

This app allows you to listen to email instead of reading it, and send email by using your voice. This can be particularly useful if you are driving and have a headset and microphone. Simply listen to your emails and reply to any of them you choose by issuing voice commands.

# Best App for Free Telephony

## Skype
**Free**
**Version: 1.0.0.5**
**Skype, Ltd.**

If you find yourself connected to a wireless router and want to make a call to someone overseas, why not do it with Skype? It's free, it's reliable, and it's good quality. You can call anyone who has a Skype account for free, and you can pay to call people who are on a landline or cell phone. You may wonder why you'd use Skype on a phone at all. Suppose you're making an international call. Or perhaps you're traveling with Wi-Fi but no cellular signal. In either case, fire up Skype and you'll be all set to make calls for free or cheap.

**CONTACT MANAGEMENT:** Skype's contact management feature lets you quickly dial and contact your friends on Skype. Just as in the desktop version, this app shows you who is online at any time. From the menu screen, you can also set your status to busy, in a meeting, or whatever you choose if you prefer not to be bothered.

**CALL OR CHAT?:** Should you call or send a message? You can do both. Send a quick message to a contact who is online, and ask if they have time for a call. Just click on the person's name and you will be prompted to Call, Chat, Show Profile, Remove, or Block. If you decide to dial someone on their phone, this app will use Google Voice to complete your call.

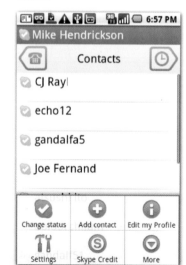

# Best App to Consolidate Your Phones

## Google Voice

**Free**
**Version: 0.3.0**
**Google, Inc.**

Google Voice (invitation only at the time of this writing) gives you a single phone number that rings all your phones, saves your voicemail online, and transcribes your voicemail to text. Other features include listening in on messages while they are being left, recording calls, making low-cost international calls, recording custom greetings for your favorite callers, and blocking annoying callers by marking them as spam. These options have always been available via the web client, but this app finally brings the full feature set to your Android phone.

**DIAL OUT:** Google Voice has always been able to connect your phone through the web client (it rings both your phone and the person you're calling), but the Android app actually lets you dial out from your Google Voice number on your handset. This makes your Google Voice number show up on caller ID and gives you amazing rates for long-distance calls. For example, I could call my friend in Australia for $.03 per minute.

**VISUALIZE YOUR VOICEMAIL:** When you can't answer, specify whether you want your regular voicemail to pick up on one of your phones, or let Google Voice take over to give you a recording and a text transcription. Transcription isn't perfect (see the fourth message), but it's good enough to give you the drift of the message. Your inbox also contains any SMS messages sent to your Google Voice number which is handy for seeing all of your voice and text messages at a glance.

83

# Best App for Analyzing Your Calls

## Phonalyzr
**Free**
**Version: 1.2**
**Martin Drashkov**

Phonalyzr displays your call log and SMS log information in a variety of groupings and graphs. This is a handy way to keep track of your plan's minutes if you're not concerned about going over your limit. You can also set your billing date range and view your history. I find it interesting to look at the top Callers by Calls chart, so I can see who I am talking with the most.

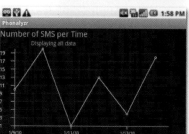

## Faves
**Free / $1.99 Full version**
**Version: 2.1**
**EyeOnWeb**

Faves is similar to Phonalyzr, but has fewer charts and visual elements. It displays your call logs in a nice table that is sortable and searchable. When you dive into a log for a particular contact, you have the option to get Contact Information, Call Log, Trends, or Clear Data. The Trends option allows you to view a chart detailing your log history with basic stuff like the caller, including Time, In Calls, and Out Calls.

Communication

# Best Phone Silencing App

## Shut the (Phone) Up
$0.99
Version: 2.0.1
DroidRepair

Have you ever forgotten to turn off your phone, and then been mortified when it began to ring at the worst possible time? It's happened to the best of us. With the STFU app, just lay your phone face-down and it won't make a sound. You can also program the phone to either vibrate or become completely silent when it is placed in a horizontal position or at an angle. If you select the large angle, you can drop your phone in your bag at about a 90 degree angle and get it to turn off.

**SIMPLE OPTIONS:** You can set STFU to activate at three main angles (no angle, slight angle, large angle), and choose one of the two modes (vibrate and silent). That's all there is to it!

 **HONORABLE MENTION**

## Ringtone Scheduler
Free
Version: v2.61
Fan Zhang

Tired of being woken up by a wrong number on a Sunday morning? The Ringtone Schedule app lets you control whether you want ringtones or silence according to the time and the days of the week. Just set your rules and enjoy your quiet time.

# Best App for Using Bluetooth

## Bluetooth File Transfer
**Free**
**Version: 2.40**
**Medieval Software**

Another way for you to communicate is with Bluetooth, which allows you to connect to hands-free devices or share files between computers. With this app, you can use Bluetooth file transfer methods such as OBEX to exchange files with a computer or device that you have paired with. In addition to sharing files with devices with Bluetooth, this app excels at sharing contact information from your address book.

**LOCAL BROWSING:** The Bluetooth File Transfer lets you browse your local files and click the ones you want to send to another device. You can also share folders and directories; highlighting the top-level folder will transfer all the files within.

**REMEMBER YOUR CONNECTIONS:** It's easy to access the main navigation to your desktop through the Bookmarks, Recent, or Found menu items. The app remembers all your connections, so after you've connected to your computer the first time, it's a snap to do it again.

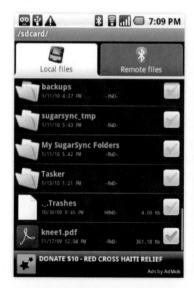

# Best App for Not Communicating

## Secret Box
**Free**
**Version: 1.0.8**
**gnugu**

Even in this age of near-constant sharing, there are still things you want to keep to yourself. This app is like a secret lock box that is protected by a password. As a quick security test, I used the Android Software Developer Kit (SDK) to transfer one of the files in the Secret Box to my laptop and confirmed that it was encrypted and could not be viewed without the password. You can even encrypt pictures, so you can store a picture of a legal document in the box as well. My one concern is that the name "Secret Box" itself could draw the attention of a would-be hacker or thief.

**SIMPLE INPUT:** This is a straightforward app, and there's not much to it except good, secure protection for data and pictures. It is very easy to add new items: first, you add compartments, and then you put items inside the compartments. For instance, I have a Pass compartment that contains four passwords I use for various websites.

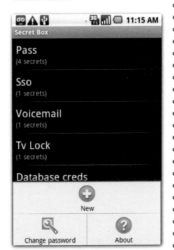

 HONORABLE MENTION

## Phone Recorder
**Free**
**Version: 1.2.0**
**Mamoru Tokashiki**

The Phone Recorder app lets you record conversations as they are happening. (Be sure to let the person on the other end of the line know that you are recording.) The app records for 10 minutes at a time and saves the last 5 minutes. I often use this for recording and playing back ski reports that I want to share with family members.

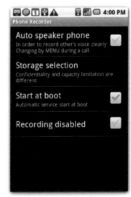

87

# Best App for Social Communication

## AnyPost
**Free**
Version: 1.12
skAmped, Ltd.

If you are like most people, you have accounts on several social networks such as Facebook, Twitter, MySpace, LinkedIn, FriendFeed, Plaxo, Plurk, and others. In fact, you may already use Ping.fm to update your status on all of them from one place. You can do the same thing from your phone using the AnyPost app, which uses the Ping.fm APIs to update all your social networks with one post. You can also post pictures from this app, and include your GPS location in your posting.

**EFFECTIVE TIME-SAVER:** If you consistently update your social network sites, you will love this app. All you need is a Ping.fm account, and then you can use this app to post your message to all the accounts you've configured with Ping.fm. The app has a very simple interface that lets you get your post out quickly.

**POST AWAY:** AnyPost offers nine major networks that you can post to. You can highlight one or all of your networks, and you can have a map link sent with your post with a simple click in your settings. You can also limit the size of your photo attachments so your post uploads quickly.

Communication

# HelloTXTroid

**Free**
**Version: 1.5**
**Buongiorno**

The HelloTXTroid app makes it easy to keep in touch with your friends on different social networks that are fed from hellotxt.com. Much like AnyPost, this app lets you update all your accounts from one place, although you do need to first set up and configure your account from the Web. It's simple to set up, easy to run, and powerful enough to make things go lightning-fast once you are up and running. HelloTXTroid is not quite as full-featured as AnyPost, but it's still an excellent all-in-one social network posting app.

**SIMPLE STEPS:** Once you set up your account and configure your settings, you're good to go. Click the upper-left tab to write your post, click the camera icon to take a picture (or include one from your SD card), and then click Update. It's as easy as one, two, three.

**SEE YOUR TIMELINE:** HelloTXTroid can bring back all the messages found on your social networks and display them in chronological order. To see your messages, click on the upper-right tab and your messages will be displayed in a list. Clicking a message allows you to read it in a pop-up window, but you can't reply to or forward it.

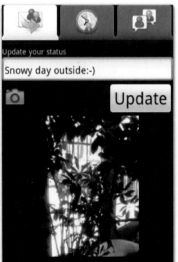

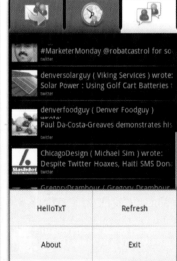

# Best Facebook App

## Facebook for Android

**Free**
**Version: 1.1.2**
**Facebook**

This app makes it easy to stay in touch with your Facebook friends, post status updates, adjust user settings, and most everything else you want to do with Facebook. Set the refresh interval to conserve your battery, and choose how you want to be notified of new Messages, Pokes, Requests, Events, and Invites. One nice feature is that if you click and hold on a message, you are prompted to choose Comment or Like, View Profile, or view any URLs in the message.

**CLEAN INTERFACE:** When you fire up this app, you're presented with six options; click on one and you'll get the latest news from that area of your Facebook account. I actually like this app better than the web version of Facebook—it's cleaner and not so cluttered with ads. I also love the news feed because I have fewer friends on Facebook than I do on Twitter, so I can see the posts from my Facebook friends better because there is less noise.

**DIVE IN:** This app will take you deep into your Facebook account. Some of the activities will take place inside this app, whereas others will redirect you to the mobile web version of Facebook. The quick ability to comment or give a thumbs up ("like") is really nice if you like to stay active with your friends. If you click on a photo, you will be taken to the image and others that are in that Facebook library.

# BFF Photo-Facebook Upload

**Free**
**Version: 1.91**
**Carmen Delessio**

This simple but powerful app is great if you enjoy sharing and viewing photos on Facebook. It's easy to view all your friends' photos on your phone, and your own photos as well. In addition, you can shoot and upload both photos and videos directly from your phone. When viewing a photo, it's easy to Save to Gallery, which will save the file locally on your SD card. If you like posting your photos on Facebook and exploring all your friends' photos, this is a worthy app to install on your phone.

**SINGLE PURPOSE:** This app doesn't try to do too much—the developers have stuck to the central idea of uploading and viewing photos or videos, and the app does this very well. You can also add simple tags to your uploads and can save locally, but that's about it. No fancy editing tools here.

**TAP THROUGH:** In addition to using the the Back/Next arrows, you can also simply tap the screen to advance to the next photo in the album. If you tap the screen outside the photo, the app brings up any captions that may be associated with the photo.

# Best App for News Feeds

## FeedR News Reader

Free demo / $0.99
Version: 1.0.3
Weekend Coders, LLC

What's not to love about an app that allows you to find feeds and news you want to load on your phone without having to type a bunch of URLs? The Feed Search is powered by Google, and is an awesome way to discover the news sources you want. And once you find your sources, you can create shortcuts so you have one-touch access to your feeds. You can fine-tune your feeds by loading them through Google, which will help clean up oddly formatted feeds. It's an excellent way to get all your news on the go.

**MIX AND MATCH:** I typically read tech-related feeds, but I also love baseball, football, and basketball. With this app you can combine all your varied interests into one place and view your personalized news. To add more feeds, simply click the Add tab and search for what you want. The search uses Google to find the most appropriate RSS feeds and returns a list of results.

**OPTIONS AND MORE:** This app gives you tons of options, so you can customize it to bring back exactly what you want. You can control how frequently you poll for feeds, so if you want to save your battery, choose a longer interval, like every 24 hours. You can also back up and restore your feed lists, which is handy if you want to share your list. Just find the *.opml* file on the SD card.

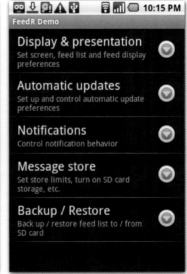

# NewsRob
**Free / €3.99 Pro version**
**Version: 3.5.0**
**Mariano Kamp**

NewsRob is a solid newsreader that syncs with Google Reader to bring you the news feeds you have selected. You can set it to return from 50 to 1,000 of the most recent articles. One nice feature is that you can mark your news items as either read or unread, and unlike with other readers, the next time you sync to get more articles, NewsRob downloads only the unread articles and deletes the read articles from your phone to make room for more. In fact, when I come across a group of articles I don't want to read, I just mark them all as "read" so they disappear from my feed on the next sync.

**DOWNLOAD EVERYTHING:** This app does a nice job of downloading everything from the article, including images, links, videos, and so on. This is particularly nice if you want to save a picture. NewsRob lets you star items so you can quickly find them later. You can also share a link to an item.

**MANAGE FEEDS:** If you click Menu, choose More, and then select Manage Feeds, you will be able to set download preferences for a particular feed. The options are Headers Only, Feed Content, Feed + Mobile Web Page, and Feed + Web Page. You can also set a notification for this feed to alert you when new articles come in.

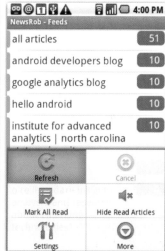

# Best Lifestyle Apps

Your Android phone is more than just a powerful tool to keep your business life running—it's a touchstone for your **hobbies** and **passions**. Like a good friend who knows you well, your phone can serve as a lifestyle advisor. Moreover, you can tailor it to give you direction for the areas of your life that matter most.

In this chapter, you'll find apps that help you live the life you want, fulfilling your personal resolutions and making your phone **adapt to your environment**, outlook, and lifestyle. First, get in shape with apps for **training**, **exercising**, and just **keeping fit**. Then, find out the most convenient and inexpensive way to **book your travel** and **record the details of your trip** for yourself and your friends. Make sure the weather is appropriate for that vacation, and learn where to **shop** more **ethically, efficiently,** and **affordably** while you're away.

Of course you live most of your life at home, so you need apps for entertaining, from **cocktail recipes** and **food dishes** to **organizing your wardrobe**. Find stuff you need, from a **new home** or **apartment** to your **lost car** or **phone**, or even a **bathroom** when you really have to go. You can even turn your phone into a **metal detector** to find that lost paperclip on your desk. Finally, you'll find the best ways to **organize all this stuff** and actually **get it done**. After installing the apps in this chapter and taking them through their paces, your phone will know more about you than most of your closest friends. Ask it the right questions and it will likely offer you better recommendations to suit your lifestyle than your pals have ever known.

# Best App for Running

## My Tracks
Free
Version: 1.08
Google

Hardcore runners no longer need to shell out hundreds of dollars for an expensive GPS watch. If you have a GPS-enabled Android phone, you can get most of the same features for free with Google's My Tracks. My Tracks records and displays your distance, duration, elevation, pace, and other information in real time while you run (or ride, or hike). Even better, it integrates with Google Docs and Google Maps to record all of your running data so you can show off to your friends.

**RUNNING IN THE BACKGROUND:** My Tracks records your distance, speed, elevation, and even your latitude/longitude while you run, and displays the data on an easy-to-read interface. After the run, choose "Send to Google ..." to import your stats into a spreadsheet on Google Docs. Each run gets its own row with these details and more, allowing all sorts of data wrangling and number crunching for the most neurotic of runners.

**MY MAPS:** When you choose "Send to Google..." you also have the option to upload your route information to Google's My Maps. Each run gets its own map, linked to a field in the Google Docs spreadsheet. The map also provides thumbtack markers for points along the route (added by you or somewhat arbitrarily by default) and a summary of the stats associated with the route on Google Docs.

# Buddy Runner
**Free**
**Version: 1.5.0**
**Cooloud**

Like My Tracks, Buddy Runner tracks your distance, duration, and pace while you run, and also records elevation, route, distance, and other stats to review later, either on your phone or uploaded to your personal dashboard at *buddyrunner.com*. Buddy Runner even records calories burned and one piece of important training data My Tracks doesn't: mile splits, which is much more useful than a final average pace. Still, Buddy Runner doesn't give you the data-crunching possibilities offered by My Tracks through Google Docs.

**PACE ME:** Record your speed, duration, calories burned, and distance as you run. After uploading your stats to your personal dashboard on the Buddy Runner website, you'll get even more details and ways to view your data, including your average speed, pace splits for miles, and an elevation map. You can even integrate directly with Twitter and Facebook to automatically share your run details as soon as they're uploaded.

**ON THE MAP:** Buddy Runner plots your route with a high level of accuracy using Google Maps. When you upload your workout, the map displays on the same page with your other stats, providing a single at-a-glance view into just about everything you'd consider tracking for a particular run.

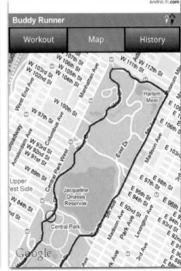

# Best Fitness App

## CardioTrainer

Free / $2.99 Full version
Version: 2.0.0
WorkSmart Labs, Inc.

CardioTrainer goes beyond just running—it's your virtual training partner for cycling, hiking, skiing, and pretty much any other outdoor activity you care to record. Your GPS gives Cardio-Trainer your real-time position, live details on your workout, and a map of your route, all of which you can push to the CardioTrainer servers to access online. Social exercisers can share training goals and progress through Facebook integration, providing powerful extrinsic motivation.

**TAKE A HIKE:** Hiking is just one of many preset workout types you can choose when you start recording your exercise (there's also skating, rollerblading, snowboarding, team sports, walking, horseback riding, and more). CardioTrainer tracks your steps, distance, elevation climb, speed, calories burned, and location, and displays your stats in real time.

**DON'T GET LOST:** The map displays your route, distance, steps, and workout duration. It also shows your elevation in graphical (rather than numeric) format. Zoom in for closer detail, or view your entire route by scaling back. Of course, location awareness requires a strong GPS or 3G signal, so keep that in mind for those hikes in the middle of nowhere.

# SportyPal

**Free**
**Version: 1.6.1**
**CreationPal**

SportyPal also logs more exercises than just running, but it comes with fewer built-in workout types than Cardio-Trainer, relegating activities other than running, walking, cycling, and roller-blading to a catchall "Free Style" category. Also, unlike CardioTrainer, it doesn't work as a pedometer (step counter), though most of its other functionality is the same and displayed in a slightly prettier interface.

**WORKING OUT:** Choose from a variety of workouts before starting to sweat, and SportyPal will keep a record of your workout history for each activity. Starting a workout is as easy as selecting the workout type and pressing Start. You'll immediately see the clock start ticking away, which means it's time to get a move on.

**GEEK MY RIDE:** Chart your bike ride (or run, walk, skate, or whatever) in real time. But please, don't start analyzing your stats when you're pedaling along at top speed. You'll have plenty of time to pore over the details when they're sent online, but if you need an immediate update, pull over. This app can definitely turn into a dangerous distraction on the road without some basic safety precautions.

# Best Travel-Booking App

## Kayak

**Free**
**Version: 0.3.12**
**Kayak**

Kayak.com is one of the largest travel search sites, and this app brings its flight, hotel, car rental, and other trip searches to your Android phone in a clean, easy-to-navigate interface. Like the website it integrates with, the Kayak app sifts through the data from hundreds of different travel sites, allowing you to compare options, prices, and more before sending you off to book your trip in whatever manner you want, whether it's at the airline site, the hotel, a car rental company, or a travel agent.

**CHOOSE YOUR ADVENTURE:** Kayak's main screen lets you tailor your search to find exactly what you're looking for, whether it's picking a flight, reserving a hotel, renting a car, checking your flight status, or getting information on flight trends. (Click the Buzz icon for best fares and average fare details between specific locations over a certain time frame.)

**TAKE FLIGHT:** The Flight screen allows you to narrow down your options to find the perfect match for your trip. Choose your origin and destination, the dates you're planning to travel, and your cabin preference (Economy, Business, or First Class). You can also specify a one-way trip or a nonstop flight.

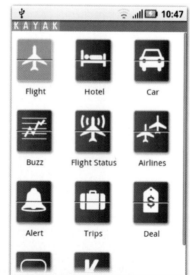

Lifestyle

# Best App for Plotting Your Travels

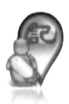

## 8Footprints

Free
Version: 1.6.6.1
Apofa, Inc.

Leave your mark on the map of the places you visit by plotting events, special occasions, and memories in the locations where they happen. With 8Footprints, you can save a "footprint"—a picture, note, or personal audio record—to a public map (you can also set the footprint as private). The service also records environmental data, so you'll have a record of exactly how cold and rainy it was for that outdoor wedding in Seattle you planned so carefully.

**LEAVE ONLY FOOTPRINTS:** Put yourself on the map with a brief note, photo, or dictation. Check in to let everyone know where you are, and in the future you can look back on your own historical timeline. You have the option to set the footprint to private, but wouldn't it be more fun to announce your footprint with Twitter and let viewers send you a friendly SMS message?

**MEET YOUR NEIGHBORS:** View the map of the location surrounding your footprint and search for people who have also recently checked in. This can be a great way to get to know people with similar interests who live right down the street from you but whom you've never met. Follow in their footprints and introduce yourself!

# Best App for Living Green

## Find Green

Free
Version: 1.0
3rdWhale Media Inc.

Living green isn't always easy, at least without a little help. Sure, you can buy local produce at the farmers' market and ride your bike to work, but what about all the other stuff you need? How green is the retail store down the street, and could you find a more responsible alternative? Find Green is here to help with everyday decisions like these, enabling you to reduce your environmental impact by easily identifying green and sustainable businesses.

**GREENER PASTURES:** Drill down to find the greenest of businesses for just about any category, within walking distance or a short drive or bike ride away. The subcategory changes based on the parent category, providing plenty of options. Find Green uses your location to determine the closest matches and returns them as a list or as pushpins on a map.

**IT'S NOT EASY BEING GREEN:** Finding green businesses is a challenging task, so much so that you might be forgiven if you've thrown up your hands in defeat just thinking about it. Until now. You probably never knew there was an environmentally friendly cabinet maker just a short drive away, but now you do, and you can get directions, visit the company's website, or give them a call with just one tap on your phone.

# Best Pet Care App

## Pet Care Services

**Free**
**Version: 1.2**
**Michael Quach**

Your pet is an important member of your family, so of course you take him with you on vacation, right? But when you're away from home, you're also removed from your trusted pet care services. Whether your dog needs a shampoo, sitter, walker, dog park, day care, trainer, emergency veterinary care, or just that certain brand of dog food that's the only thing he'll eat, Pet Care Services puts you in touch with the closest providers.

**HERE COME THE GROOMERS:** If Fido rolls around in the muck when you visit the family farm, where are you going to take your pooch to get cleaned up professionally? A quick search reveals there are more groomers in the area than you realized, faster and more efficiently than sifting through Google results or (gasp!) flipping through the Yellow Pages.

**PET PROJECTS:** Select a provider from the list to see exactly where they're located. Send yourself an email or text message with the address, or just give them a call by pressing the phone icon on your screen.

# Best Shopping App

## ShopSavvy
**Free**
**Version: 3.6.0**
**Big in Japan, Inc.**

So you're standing in the tissue aisle at the local market, wondering why Kleenex is so expensive today. Is it a new product that people really love? Or could it just be labeled incorrectly? Maybe it's cheaper at the grocery store down the street? Before you head to the checkout line, scan its barcode with ShopSavvy for immediate answers to these questions. You'll get comparisons, reviews, and prices at other local or on-line stores, so you can be sure to get the best deal on that Kleenex.

**BUY WHERE YOU SHOP:** You find the book you want in a major chain bookstore, but would really prefer to spend your money at your beloved independent shop. The first thing you need to know is whether the mom and pop store has the book in stock, and then you can decide if buying from them is worth it to you. ShopSavvy tells you the prices at the local competition and finds you the best deals online.

**THE REVIEWS ARE IN:** Can't make a decision on whether to buy that book you're holding at the bookstore? Why not find out what other people thought about it? ShopSavvy provides on-the-spot customer reviews in a clean format, without making you type the title into a search box and sift through other product information on your small screen.

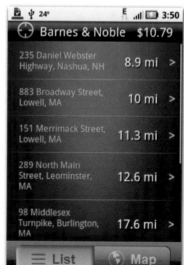

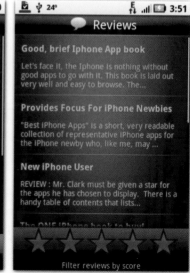

# Best Rewards Card App

## Key Ring
## Reward Cards

Free
Version: 1.3.5
Froogloid, LLC

Is your key ring or wallet overflowing with all the rewards cards (also known as affinity cards) you've collected from the supermarket, hotel, drugstore, hardware store, frequent flyer programs, bookstore, rental car company, and other stores or service providers? Organize them all in one place with Key Ring Reward Cards. With all your barcodes on your phone, you'll never need to carry another card again.

**ONE KEY RING TO RULE THEM ALL:** Just start scanning your barcodes and loading them up on your Key Ring. If your card is so old or beat up that your phone can't read the barcode, don't worry. Just select the retailer from the huge list of options and enter the number on the barcode manually.

**SWIPE THIS:** When the person at the checkout asks for your rewards card, select the retailer from your Key Ring list, hand over the phone, and tell the cashier to swipe your screen. The virtual card might get you a raised eyebrow, but it'll work just as well as the physical card that used to take up space in your wallet.

# Best App for Food Recipes

## Favorite Recipes

**Free**
**Version: 2.2.0**
**Favorite Android**

How many cookbooks can you fit in your kitchen? How about in your pocket? With Favorite Recipes on your phone, you can search thousands of recipes by ingredient, keyword, or category without ever having to flip through a book or prop open pages. Whether you're rediscovering your traditional favorites or seeking out something new, you'll find something for every occasion and palate with this simple and easy-to-use interface.

**HUNT AND GATHER:** Each search returns 50 random results for the term or phrase you enter. Whether you have a unique ingredient in your fridge that you want to work into a dish or you know exactly what you want to make, you should find the recipe you're looking for. Keep in mind that you'll be drawing from a huge database of recipes, so for best results, be as specific as possible with your request.

**NOW WE'RE COOKING:** Favorite Recipes doesn't provide pictures, but the ingredients list and detailed instructions should give you a pretty good idea of what to expect. Just make sure your fingers are clean and dry before you scroll down to continue reading; there's nothing like olive oil on your screen to frustrate your cooking experience.

# Best App for Cocktail Recipes

## 10001 Cocktails

Free
Version: 4.1
Red Droid Software

This pocket bartender will be your secret weapon for your next cocktail party. Your guest wants a Clam Digger? Another wants a Pedro Collins? Someone else just wants something fancy with tequila? No problem. Play it cool and give your guests exactly what they want. You can browse preloaded recipes or search the website by alcohol category, ingredient, or drink name. You may forget names, but you'll never forget another drink.

PICK YOUR POISON: Search an alphabetical list of drinks, browse by drink type, search for ingredients or drink names, and save your favorites for future reference. You even get a lame random pickup line on the home screen, though you're sure to have better results with the recipes.

SHAKEN, NOT STIRRED: Cocktail recipes are stripped down to their essence with basic ingredients, to-the-point instructions for mixing, and user ratings. Of course, use your own judgment and taste when creating your masterpiece, and be willing to accommodate special requests. Still, do you really think James Bond could tell the difference between shaken and stirred?

# Best Real Estate App

## Real Estate Droid
**Free**
**Version: 2.0.7**
**Awesome Android Apps**

If you're in the market for a new home, give this app a spin before you consult a real estate agent. You can search for homes in your price range and desired location, estimate home values with Zillow, and get neighborhood information from Trulia, Walkscore, and Rentometer, based on your location. When you think you're ready to buy, crunch the numbers with the built-in mortgage quotes and loan calculator. Your dream home might be just a few clicks away.

**HOUSE SEARCH:** What's your price range? Narrow your search to include only homes you can afford, specify how many bedrooms and bathrooms you need, and limit your results to a particular city or surrounding neighborhoods (based on distance from your first choice).

**LITTLE BOXES:** Your search returns all the homes matching your criteria; if your choices are broad, this could be an awfully long list. Press Back to narrow your search, or choose a house based on the summary info (address, price, square footage, a thumbnail photo, and number of bedrooms and bathrooms) for more photos and details.

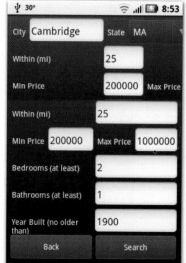

Lifestyle

# Best Mortgage Calculator

## Mortgage Calculator

Free / $.99 Pro version
Version: 4.2.0
Siva G

You've found your dream home and know how much you can afford. You've talked to a lender and have a good idea of what you'll be able to get for an interest rate. Pull out Mortgage Calculator on the spot to see exactly what you're looking at. Though Real Estate Droid offers a built-in mortgage calculator, this dedicated app is packed with advanced features, including amortization. The Pro version includes fine-grained payment options and a refinance calculator.

ADD IT UP: Advanced mode lets you include the property value, down payment, insurance options, taxes, and other expenses in your calculation. If you're just looking for a quick ballpark estimate, use the default mode, which calculates monthly payment based on loan amount, term (in years), and interest rate.

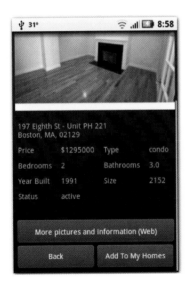

HOME SWEET HOME: Could this be the one? Get more information and pictures with one click, or add the home to your watch list for comparison later. Use this app to organize your house-hunting tour.

# Best App for Apartment Hunting

## Apartments

**Free**
**Version: 2.1**
**David Quinlan**

Need new digs but not ready to buy? Use this app to tap into the thousands of available rentals listed at ApartmentGuide.com, with the extra features only a mobile app can provide. Take it along on your hunt and use the GPS feature to find apartments near you. Collect properties in your favorites to compare later on. When you're ready to set up an appointment to view, select a property and call or email the rental office with one touch.

**PADS IN YOUR HOOD:** Search by location, either based on your current GPS fix or a zip code you've specified, and you'll get a complete list of available properties in the area. When available, each entry includes a thumbnail photo, address, pricing, and number of bedrooms.

**ROOM WITH A VIEW:** The Property Details screen provides a description of the unit; pricing information; square footage; number of bedrooms; features of the building, community, or apartment; and any pet policy. If the building has more than one apartment available, the floor plan and price are provided for each unit. You can also conveniently check availability or call the rental office directly from this screen.

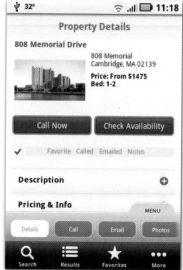

# Best Fashion Organizing App

## MyCloset

**Free**
**Version: 1.1.0**
**Mamoru Tokashiki**

If you can never decide what to wear or find yourself forgetting about that sweater in the back of the closet that doesn't go with anything, it's time to organize your closet. But instead of going out and buying space savers, shoe racks, and extra hangers, use MyCloset to manage information about your clothes virtually. Catalog your entire wardrobe, select an outfit without digging through racks of clothes, and record your daily outfits for posterity.

**CLOSET ORGANIZER:** Take control of your wardrobe by organizing all of your fashion items in MyCloset. Start by either taking a photo of each piece, choosing from preloaded items, or importing information from *myclo.com*. Give your item a name, index it by color, and specify which seasons it's appropriate for.

**CLOSET COORDINATES:** What do you have that goes with that green sleeveless top you want to wear today? Open MyCloset to coordinate your whole outfit, matching tops, bottoms, outerwear, shoes, accessories, even handbags. The zipper that you use to scroll down all the categories is a particularly nice touch.

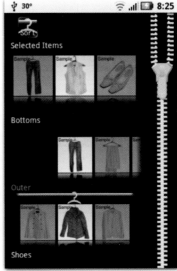

# Best App for Finding Your Car

## Carrr Matey

**Free**
**Version: 1.5.9**
**Lionebra Studios**

Dude, where's my car? With Carrr Matey on your phone, you'll never have to ask that question again. Mark your position when you park, and Carrr Matey will guide you back using a compass or walking directions. While you're at it, if you're feeding a meter, go ahead and set the timer. You'll know not just how to get back in your car, but also *when* you need to be there.

DROP ANCHOR: When you leave your car, drop your anchor to establish your position. You can zoom in or out, so you'll be able to find your car whether it's just outside in the parking lot or miles away at the hotel you've forgotten the name of.

WE HAVE OUR HEADING: Turn on the compass on your way back to get pointed in the right direction, or get walking directions for more precision. Keep in mind, however, that this app requires a GPS fix to determine your location, so if you're in an underground parking garage or other place with no signal, you're out of luck.

# Best App for Finding Your Phone

## Pintail

**Free**
**Version: 1.0.2**
**Tom Gibara**

Have you ever lost your phone, or worried that it may have been stolen? Find out exactly where it is by sending a text message from any other phone. Pintail keeps track of your phone's position, and when you send your phone an SMS message that includes your personal PIN, Pintail will send back its location. If you want to share your location with friends or family, just give them your PIN number and they can keep tabs on you without having to call and ask where you are.

**PIN A TAIL ON YOUR PHONE:** Setting your phone up with Pintail is as easy as launching the app and entering a PIN at the prompt. You can change your PIN at any time by opening the app again, so if you've temporarily shared your location with friends or family for a specific reason, you can easily make the PIN private.

**PHONE HOME:** When you find your phone has gone missing, borrow someone else's phone (or use an online SMS service) and send a text message with the text "locate *<PIN>*" to your phone. Pintail will find your phone's position and return a text message with an estimate of its location, complete with a link to Google Maps.

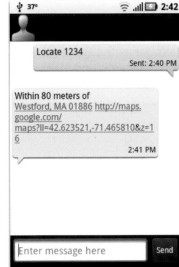

# Best App for Finding an ATM

## Bank & ATM Finder
Free
Version: 1.3
Michael Quach

Short on cash in unfamiliar territory? Bank & ATM Finder uses your position to find the closest ATMs and bank branches, as well as offering search filters for other places to get cash advances, cash checks, purchase a money order, transfer money, or secure a payday loan. As long as you have your phone with you (and money in your checking account), you never need to worry about being stranded without cash again.

**GET CASH FAST:** Bank & ATM Finder returns a list of the cash machines closest to you, listed in order of proximity and labeled with both the machine's location and its distance from your current position.

**MAP IT:** When you select the bank location you want to get to, Bank & ATM Finder displays the address on a map. Choose the up arrow to launch Google Maps and get driving directions, send yourself a text message or email with a link to the map, or give the bank a call by pressing the phone icon.

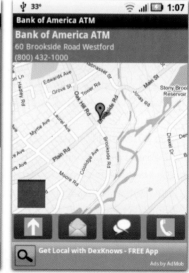

Lifestyle

# Best App for Finding a Bathroom

## SitOrSquat

Free
Version: 1.2
Densebrain, Inc.

When you gotta go, you gotta go. But if you've ever tried finding a public restroom in downtown Boston, for example, you know you can end up holding it a long time without a little help. This app accesses the 73,000 restrooms, toilets, and bathrooms around the world users have registered and rated on the *SitOrSquat.com* wiki. Search for the closest cans to your location, or specify an address to find the right one for you.

**WHEN NATURE CALLS:** When the need to find a bathroom hits, choose My Location to get a map of the public toilets nearby. If you're planning a trip where the bathrooms are notoriously hard-to-find (or if your GPS can't find a signal), you can search by any address to get the same map.

**TOILET DETAILS:** Choose a possible restroom venue to learn more details, including the precise location of the bathroom in the building, the proprietor's phone number, and a website if the business has one. You'll also see user ratings that rank the toilet as clean ("sit") or dirty ("squat"). After your experience, you can share your own reviews at *SitOrSquat.com*, but you'll have to do it on the Web—that feature isn't offered in this version of the mobile app.

# Best Weather App

## WeatherBug
**Free / $1.99 Elite version**
**Version: 2.2.79**
**WeatherBug Mobile**

When you want a detailed weather report presented in an attractive interface, call on WeatherBug. You'll get current conditions, extended forecasts, maps, photos, and emergency weather alerts. For $1.99, the Elite version removes the ads and adds map layers, a location summary screen, a forecast widget, and a few other features; however, for all but the most weather obsessed, the free version provides as much information as you'd ever want to know.

**CURRENT CONDITIONS:** If you just want to know the current temperature, look on the left side of your status bar. Pull down the shade for a few more details, and select the notification to launch the full version of WeatherBug, with complete details of current conditions, including wind, humidity, dew point, pressure, and more. If there's a webcam in the area, you might also get to see a picture by pressing the camera icon.

**WEEKLY FORECAST:** Press the calendar icon at the bottom of the screen to get a summary view of the week ahead in weather. Choose any day to slide away the rest of the week and get the forecast for that particular day. Press the exclamation point for storm watches, wind advisories, and other emergency notifications; when issued, these will also appear in your status bar.

# The Weather Channel

**Free**
**Version: 2.1.9**
**The Weather Channel**

The Weather Channel app draws on data from *Weather.com* to offer pretty much the same features as WeatherBug, including current conditions, maps, and extended forecast. Its forecast goes a little further by showing 10 days into the future (WeatherBug shows a week of forecasts), and finer with an hourly forecast that WeatherBug lacks. But it does everything with so much less style (rigid layout, no animated transitions, etc.) that it makes weather look as boring as most people think it is.

**WEATHER NOW:** Putting function before form, the Weather Channel app provides all the detail you need for current conditions. The red box with the exclamation point indicates an emergency notification (in this case, a winter storm warning); just press it to get all the gory details.

**NEXT 10 DAYS:** The Weather Channel's extended forecast goes three days further than WeatherBug's seven days, but weather forecasts for more than a week ahead don't tend to be very accurate anyway.

# Best App for To-Do Lists

## Astrid

**Free**
**Version: 2.10.1**
we <3 astrid

A handy to-do list, tracking system, and source of helpful reminders, Astrid is like having a completely reliable personal assistant in your pocket. Boost your productivity and actually get stuff done by recording and tagging action items, giving yourself deadlines, setting up alerts, and sticking to it. If you already use the online task-management service Remember the Milk, you'll be able to seamlessly sync your to-do lists with Astrid.

**STAY ON TASK:** If you're looking for ways to get things done more effectively, it often helps to give yourself a deadline when you enter a new task. Better yet, set a goal for getting it done, set another drop-dead absolute deadline, and specify reminder alerts for each date. On the Basic screen, give your task a name, priority, and tags (such as "work" or "family").

**CHECK IT OFF YOUR LIST:** Your dashboard allows you to see all of your tasks at a glance (or as many as possible; if you have a lot you might want to search by tag). This includes all their associated deadlines, tags, and priority levels. There's nothing more satisfying than crossing a completed task off your list!

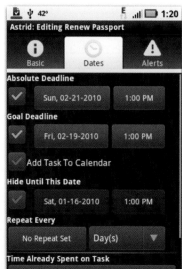

Lifestyle

# ActionComplete

Free
Version: 4.1.0
Borys Burnayev

Explicitly inspired by David Allen's productivity methodology outlined in *Getting Things Done*, ActionComplete manages your scheduled tasks much like Astrid. Create an action item, tag it, assign a priority (or "weight"), set your due date, and specify your alerts. Though it offers a few fields unavailable in Astrid, they feel a little superfluous when not connected to another system, and ActionComplete doesn't sync with third-party to-do lists.

**TAKE ACTION:** When you add a new action item to ActionComplete, you can assign it to people and a larger project. These options aren't offered in Astrid, though you could easily specify this sort of information with tags or notes.

**KEEP YOUR PRIORITIES STRAIGHT:** By default, your dashboard displays all the actions you've assigned, but you can filter your results by searching for particular tags, people, places, projects, or due dates.

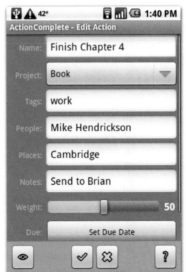

# Best Dynamic Reconfiguration App

## Locale
$9.99
Version: 0.695 beta
two forty four a.m. LLC

Is your favorite personal ringtone something you'd rather not have your officemates hear? Don't want your phone ringing at all while *Lost* is on? Once you've set conditions like these based on time, location, or the person who's calling, decide what you want to happen when those conditions are met. Just set your preferences once and Locale will manage them dynamically, automatically changing your settings based on your predefined criteria.

**A SETTING FOR EVERY SITUATION:** You know what you want your phone to do under different circumstances, so why not tell it to behave that way? Having your GPS active drains your battery quickly, so you might want to have it turn off when the battery gets below 15%. And you no longer have an excuse for having your phone ring during that weekly meeting.

**WE HAVE A SITUATION HERE:** For each situation, you can choose multiple conditions and settings. If you use Bluetooth only at work, you can have it turn on only when you're in the office. If you're usually busy during the day and need to work quietly, you can send all personal calls to voicemail from 9 to 5 or whenever you're actually in the office.

# Best Metal Detector

## Metal Detector

**Free**
**Version: 1.2**
**Kurt Radwanski**

This deceptively simple app does just one thing, but it does that one thing well, and that one thing is pretty darn cool. Using your Android phone's built-in compass as a magnetometer, Metal Detector does just what its name suggests. Sure, it doesn't have a lot of practical uses beyond finding the keys you dropped in the sand or the nail head you just painted over in the wall, but it's great for impressing friends at parties.

**A QUICK SCAN:** Because it does only one thing and has no extra options, Metal Detector gets right to work as soon as you launch it, scanning for any metal under the back of your phone. Move slowly over the area you're scanning and watch the progress bar as you get closer to finding what you're looking for.

**PRECIOUS METAL:** Accuracy varies, but if you move your phone slowly you're likely to detect most metals (though not aluminum or other metals without magnetic attraction). When the scan hits metal, the status bar goes completely red and your phone will vibrate. Show it off to a group of impressionable friends and it'll seem like magic.

# Best App for Bird Watching

## iBird Explorer Pro
$29.99
Version: 1.0
Mitch Waite Group

Bird watchers and amateur ornithologists with Android phones no longer need to be jealous of their iPhone-carrying friends, who've already been using the app that Macworld awarded Best Reference App of 2009. The Android release of iBird Explorer is the same interactive field guide to nearly 1,000 birds of North America, featuring beautiful illustrations, photos, audio samples of bird calls, and plenty of facts to satisfy your curiosity about that bird you just spotted.

**FOR THE BIRDS:** Search by bird name, habitat, range, shape, size, and more to find the bird you're trying to identify. Each bird page features a stunning illustration and navigation to learn more about the species. If you find something close to the right bird but not quite, you might find what you're looking for in the Similar category.

**HOME ON THE RANGE:** Each bird detail page includes navigation to a range map of the bird's natural habitat. Chances are, if you're on the east coast and only California is highlighted, you've got the wrong bird. You'll also be able to hear a sample of the bird's song, view photos, and get plenty of detailed facts, from its physical characteristics to its diet and behavior.

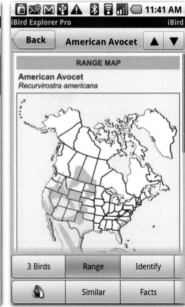

Lifestyle

# Best Augmented Reality App

## Layar Reality Browser

Free
Version: 2.0
Layar

If you thought a heads-up display that layers real-time information over the reality you're already seeing was reserved for science fiction, you haven't seen Layar. Hold the phone in front of you like a camera, select the layer to display, and watch the nearby places and objects map onto the very environment around you. Give the things in your world name tags to find businesses, people, places, or anything you'd otherwise miss with your eyes only.

**LAYER YOUR WORLD:** Choose from local, featured, or popular layers, or search for just the right layer for your situation. Once the layer is mapped over your reality, specify your search. Here I'm searching for pizza within a five-mile radius of my current location.

**MORE THAN MEETS THE EYE:** Using the phone as a viewfinder for your surroundings, check out the search results in front of you. Here we see the pizza places within a short drive of my house. Looks like most of them are straight ahead, but I think I'll turn around because there's a pizza joint behind me too.

# Best Entertainment Apps

Wherever you are, if you find yourself alone and in need of entertainment, you'll likely reach for your Android phone. This chapter will help you turn your phone into a portable entertainment center: a single device in the palm of your hand to store, access, play, edit, and share your media with others.

Film buffs will **find movies**, theaters, showtimes, and reviews for the latest flicks in the same place you check your **Netflix queue** and share DVD reviews with friends. For couch potatoes, there are apps for **TV listings** for your local area and even for **watching TV** on your phone.

Of course your phone is an MP3 player, but it can be so much more. You'll find slick apps for **playing music and video**, from your own library or from **streaming radio** and **YouTube**. If you aren't content to just consume, other apps will help you **create and distribute** your own media, from **recording audio** and **launching podcasts** to **streaming live video** to a captive audience online. Finally, you'll learn to **take better photos** and **edit them like a pro**. How's that for a rich media entertainment experience with Android?

Fender™ is the trademark of Fender Musical Instruments Corporation and is used with permission.

# Best App for Film Buffs

## Movies

**Free**
**Version: 2.3.0**
**Flixster, Inc.**

Film buffs rejoice! The Movies app for Android gives you everything you need to know in one place: DVD reviews, theater showtimes, current box office news, movie trailers, and whatever comments you and your friends have already shared about the movies you love (or hate). Share ratings with your friends through Facebook, read reviews from Rotten Tomatoes, organize your Netflix queue, buy tickets to the theater...if it has to do with movies, you can do it here.

**BOX OFFICE:** Check out all the latest box office news, from what's opening this Friday to the best moneymakers of the week. If you see something that looks interesting, click the movie poster to watch the trailer.

**LOCAL THEATERS:** Itching to go see a movie? Select the Theaters tab to get a complete list of theaters in your area, sorted by proximity to your current location. Choose a theater to see the address, phone number, and complete listing of showtimes. You can even buy tickets from within the app via *movietickets.com*.

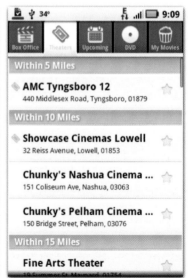

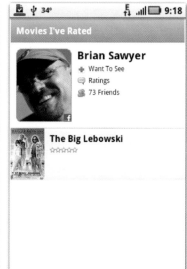

**NETFLIX QUEUE:** If you have a Netflix subscription, you'll love the way the Movies app integrates your queue. See what you're waiting for, reorder the list, add or remove movies, and remind yourself why you added a particular movie by getting photos, synopses, trailers, and more.

**MOVIES I'VE RATED:** By connecting your Facebook account to the Movies app, you can share your ratings with friends and see how your contacts have rated the movies you're checking out.

# Fandango Movies
Free
Version: 1.0.4
Fandango

If you're only interested in the movies currently playing in the theater, Fandango Movies is a great app. As with the Movies app, you can get reviews, showtimes, trailers, and box office reports, and you can even purchase tickets. But if you also watch a lot of movies at home, you'll miss the DVD features (particularly the Netflix integration) of Movies. And if you rely on your Facebook friends for ratings and reviews, you'll need to check out their walls, because Fandango doesn't talk to Facebook like the Movies app does.

# Best App for Watching TV

## TV.com

**Free**
**Version: 1.0**
**CBS Interactive, Inc.**

Want to watch the tube on the (very) small screen? If you're looking for shows offered by the CBS-owned *TV.com*, this app presents plenty of clips and a number of full-length episodes from CBS (including CBS News and CBS Sports), CW, Showtime, CNET, and more. Despite these somewhat limited options, TV.com still has a better selection of quality programming than any other mobile TV app for Android, and everything is presented in a smooth and watchable interface.

**CHANNEL SURFING:** TV.com brings you programs from channels in the CBS family only, but within those restrictions you'll find a good selection and a few gems. Most channels just offer clips, but you'll find full-length episodes of some shows from the CBS archives (*MacGyver*, *Star Trek*) and a few current shows.

**HAVING AN EPISODE:** TV.com allows you to watch entire episodes of *NCIS*, *Gossip Girl*, *Harper's Island*, *Rules of Engagement*, *60 Minutes*, *The Late Show with David Letterman*, and others. These shows also offer smaller clips, so you can watch just that one interview segment on Letterman and skip the stupid pet tricks.

# Best App for TV Listings

## TV-Guide USA
**Free / $2.99 Ad-free version**
**Version: 1.0.5**
**Jersey Productions**

You may be bummed by the limited selection of TV shows you can actually watch on your phone, but you still want to know what's on the big box that plugs into your wall, right? TV-Guide USA gives you a quick and easy peek into what's on now and what's coming up in your area, whether you get your service from a local over-the-air antenna, satellite, or a cable provider.

**ANYTHING GOOD ON?:** The default view gives listings for every channel. What's showing right now is at the top of the list; scroll down to see what's on for the rest of the day. If you're only interested in movies or sports, restrict your view using the tabs at the top of the screen.

**COMING UP:** Click on a particular show to bring up listings for that channel, along with any information on the show or episode. You can't get a summary of the news in advance (wouldn't that be nice?), but you can at least find out whether your favorite soap opera is a rerun or a new episode.

# Best Media Player

## TuneWiki

**Free / $4.99 Ad-free version**
**Version: 1.6**
**TuneWiki**

In addition to the media player that comes preloaded on your phone, the Android Market has many apps to enhance your listening or viewing experience. TuneWiki is the best of them, offering an intuitive interface to your music library, access to Internet radio through SHOUTcast or Last.fm, lyrics search, music maps, Top 50, playlists, and more. To make your experience more social, you can share your tastes and status via Blip, Twitter, or Facebook.

**SET LIST:** TuneWiki taps into the music directory and playlists already stored on your phone, letting you shuffle all songs or browse your library by artist, song title, album, or playlist. While you're listening to a song, you can add it to an existing playlist or create a new playlist for it on the fly.

**PLAY IT:** Select a song to play and you'll also get access to it in your navigation bar. TuneWiki retrieves album artwork and displays real-time lyrics, translated into over 40 languages, while the song is playing. You can even set the current track as your ringtone by pulling up the menu options.

**WATCH IT:** Built-in YouTube integration lets you find videos to watch within the media player. Search by artist or song title to get a list of matching results to play immediately. Of course, you could go straight to YouTube to do the same thing, but TuneWiki lets you add the video directly to your library, so you can keep all your music-related media organized in a single place.

# Meridian Player

**Free**
**Version: Noble 0.5.1**
**III - Romulus Urakagi Ts'ai**

Meridian is another solid media player for Android that offers some of the same features as TuneWiki (song rating, lyrics, extra track info) but doesn't tie into social media, Internet radio (an additional plug-in is required to connect with Last.fm), or YouTube video services. However, it does tap into your local video directory to play anything you have in there, which is nice. Another handy feature that you can set in your preferences pauses a track when you receive a phone call, and resumes playing automatically when you hang up.

**NOW PLAYING:** The player itself is simple and easy to use. It also sits in your navigation bar for quick access when you're doing other things while listening. As with TuneWiki, you can display album artwork, but you'll need to add it yourself.

# Best Remote Control

## Gmote

Free
Version: 2.0.4
Marc Stogaitis, Mimi Sun

Gmote turns your Android phone into a remote control for the media library on your computer. Once you've installed the Gmote server on your computer (a small download and easy setup), just launch the app from your phone, enter your password, and immediately gain wireless access to iTunes, your photo library, and any other folders you define. Then, use Gmote's on-screen navigation to play tracks on your computer. As of the 2.0 release, you can even stream songs through your phone's speaker!

**PLAY LOCAL:** With Gmote, you can browse through any of the media folders on your computer. Find and select the song or video you want to play to bring up the remote navigation. When browsing photo libraries, you'll see thumbnails along the bottom of the screen and a large view of the selected photo.

**REMOTE ACCESS:** Gmote has tons of everyday uses. Advance PowerPoint slides during presentations without having to stand by the podium. Play, pause, and fast-forward home movies from your couch. Sit the family back for a vacation slideshow from your desktop. Playing songs through your phone speaker works like magic, but the software doesn't support video playback just yet.

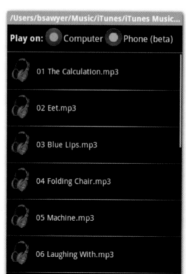

# Best Audio Management App

## AudioManager Widget

Free
Version: 1.0.6
Smart Android Apps, LLC

Whether you're playing music on your phone or just want access to all the sounds on your phone in one place, the AudioManager Widget has you covered. Like your computer's volume mixer, AudioManager gives you live readings of volume levels for each audio element of your phone. Just press and slide the volume bars to adjust each level independently. The home-screen widget gives you always-on readings, and the console for full control is just a tap away at all times.

**VOLUME CONSOLES:** AudioManager gives clear level readings for the volume of your alarms, music, alerts, ringer, system, and voice, all on a single screen. Just slide down the volume bars to reduce the annoyance of some notifications, or really pump up the volume of your tunes.

**CHOOSE YOUR WIDGET:** You have two options for the widget size. This should accommodate volume-obsessed users who want to read the titles of all their levels, and also satisfy those who just want a quick glance or can't spare the screen real estate for such detail.

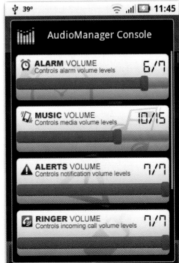

# Best Personalized Radio App

## Pandora Radio

**Free**
**Version: 1.1.2**
**Pandora**

Entertainment

Pandora is your own personalized radio, playing just the kind of songs you're interested in and helping you find new artists with similar styles. Create a unique station for each of your distinct musical tastes and tune in to whatever you're in the mood for. The more you listen, the better Pandora learns what you *really* like, providing even more targeted suggestions. If you're already a Pandora user, just log in to get immediate access to your existing personal stations.

**CREATE A STATION:** Just type the name of an artist or song you love and Pandora does the rest for you, playing songs in the same genre or artists that other users have rated similarly to your favorites. Save the station to listen to the same type of music the next time you're in the mood.

**FIND SIMILAR ARTISTS:** Which artists share a style with your favorites? You might be able to think of a few, but Pandora has enough recommendations from other users to surprise you with something new. If you agree with the recommendation, give it the thumbs up and other Pandora users will benefit from your recommendations. If Pandora got it wrong, just say so and it won't repeat the same mistake again.

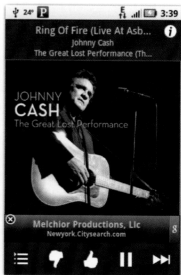

**TRACK INFO:** Never heard of an artist that Pandora suggested? Get tons of information on the artist, album, and all the traits used to associate the song with your predefined criteria.

**BUY IT NOW:** If you happen upon a new song that you just have to own, Pandora gives you one-click access to Amazon's MP3 store for immediate purchase.

 HONORABLE MENTION

# Last.fm
**Free**
**Version: 1.3.3**
**Last.fm Ltd.**

Last.fm is a very close second to Pandora, and it connects with a variety of other media players and apps through plug-ins. In fact, you'll find plenty of users who swear by Last.fm over Pandora, making the decision of which app to use largely a result of personal preference or which online service you might already use. At any rate, Last.fm definitely goes head-to-head with Pandora, feature by feature, but I have accounts with both services and find Pandora to be a slicker, more pleasing experience.

# Best Streaming Music App

## Rhapsody

**Free trial / $12.99/month subscription**
Version: 1.2
RealNetworks, Inc.

Pandora and Last.fm are great (and free) if you know what you're in the mood for but want to be surprised by the songs you get. But if you know *exactly* what you want and you want it now, go with the on-demand streaming music service offered by Rhapsody. For a monthly subscription, you'll get immediate access to millions of songs to match your whim. Rather than buying tracks or albums to remain in your collection permanently, Rhapsody gives you all the tunes you want, right now.

**BEST OF THE BEST:** Search by song or artist and see what other people are listening to most. Add songs to your queue to create a custom radio station to listen to for the rest of the day.

**NOW PLAYING:** Get album artwork and access artist information while you listen. Scroll down to see what's coming up in your queue, or skip ahead if you're already tired of the track you're on.

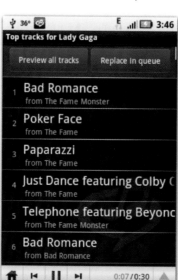

**PORTRAIT OF THE ARTIST:** Find out more about the artist of the current song with a brief history of influences, complete album list, samples of their music, their most popular songs, and related artists.

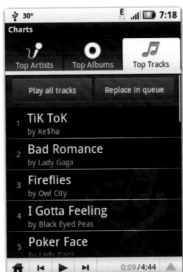

**TOP OF THE POPS:** If you're looking for the top 40, Rhapsody offers lists of the most popular artists, albums, and songs of the moment. With a constantly revolving and updating playlist of the hippest music going, you'll never miss a beat.

⊕ HONORABLE MENTION

# PlayMe

**Free trial / $9.99/month subscription**
**Version: 1.0**
**Play.me**

PlayMe is a little less expensive than Rhapsody, but its limited features make Rhapsody worth the extra three bucks a month. PlayMe does offer featured recommendations, but it doesn't offer lists of top artists, albums, and tracks, and you can't dig deep into artist information, related tracks, and other stuff offered by Rhapsody. It offers a compelling free pass, though, giving you 10 hours of music and a complimentary MP3 download per week, so it's worth giving it a spin, especially if you're not ready to shell out the dough for Rhapsody.

# Best App for Identifying Music

## Shazam
**Free**
**Version: 1.2**
**Shazam Entertainment Limited**

Do you believe in magic? Maybe you will after trying out Shazam, a jaw-droppingly awesome music identifier. If you can't place the song playing in the room at any moment, just open Shazam and tell it to listen for a few seconds. It has the uncanny ability to recognize the track and tell you pretty much anything you need to know about it. This is great for settling bar bets, and perfect for filling out all the info for your friend's mix CD that imported with helpful song names like "Track 01."

**LIKE MAGIC:** When Shazam identifies the track (as it will, more often than not, even for fairly obscure songs), it displays its "tag," which includes album artwork, title, and music label. Scroll down for more options, such as searching YouTube for the video or buying the track from Amazon's MP3 store if you've just gotta have it.

**REVIEW YOUR TAGS:** Shazam stores tags for all the songs it identifies so that you can scroll through the list later. If you find yourself grooving to all the new music in the club, just tag every song and look them up when you get home to relive the experience and perhaps even buy the soundtrack.

Entertainment

# Best Gig Guide

## Alice (Gig Guide)
Free
Version: 1.6.0
Tim Clark

So you've identified your favorite artists, streamed their music, and downloaded your favorite songs. But when are they coming to your town so you can finally see them live? Alice is an exhaustive gig guide for your Android phone, complete with maps, calendar, search, and sync with Last.fm and BandsInTown services. Just add your favorite performers to your artist watch list and get complete tour dates and notifications of when they'll be playing a venue near you.

**WATCHING AND WAITING:** Fill your watch list with the acts you'd like to see live and check in (or set alerts) to get complete tour information for each artist. The number in the pink box tells you how many shows are booked, and stars indicate events near you. Just click the artist name to get complete tour dates, listed in order of proximity.

**SAVE THE DATE:** Drill down into the event you're interested in to get details on the venue, date, distance from you, and a map of the location. When you're ready to buy your tickets, you can grab them directly through this app; you can also add the event to your calendar or email the details to your friends.

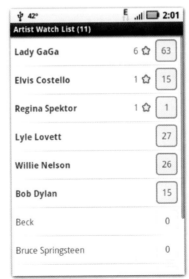

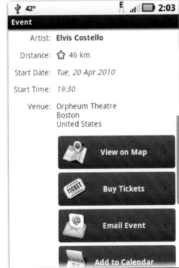

# Best Alternative Radio App

## A Online Radio

Free
Version: 0.9.8.16
aor.leadapps

This radio app has plenty of functionality that makes it easy to find your favorite music genre on radio channels around the world. Simply decide which part of the world you want to hone in on and select the type of music from that area. Once you've found your music preference, you can make it a favorite and get more information, including lyrics for the currently playing song. This app takes full advantage of Android: it keeps running when you leave it, and the green icon in your status bar lets you control it.

**SLEEP CONTROL:** My favorite feature is the ability to put your music to sleep after a preset amount of time. This means you can find a nice, mellow music channel, plug your phone into a set of speakers, and settle in for a nap, knowing that your music will stop after you fall asleep. I've been setting mine for 20 minutes and never have to turn it off.

**BROWSE THE THE CHANNELS:** There are more channels out there than you can possibly listen to. If you are trying to find your perfect channel, the search feature now accesses 10,000+ channels. This app will play SHOUTcast/Icecast-AAC and AACP channels (AAC files use the same encoding as iTunes files).

# Jamendo Player

**Free**
**Version: 0.9.8.16**
**Teleca Poland**

Jamendo Player is a frontend to the largest Creative Commons–licensed music catalog on the planet. If you want free music from independent artists, this is the app for you. Whether you're looking for a specific artist or the most frequently listened-to band, or you just want to browse through the available music, you'll find some nice options to help you get the most out of this app. I particularly like the Lyrics feature that displays the lyrics for the currently playing track.

**RADIO AND FREE MUSIC:** You have the option to search by Artist, Tag, User Playlists, or User Starred Albums. Once a search list is returned to you, you can see what other users have rated as the best songs in your search category. One click on any item in your search list will get the song playing and return all the details about the specific song.

**GREAT INTERFACE:** It's great to hear exactly what you want, but one of the best things about listening to the radio is exposure to new music. With this app, it's easy to find new stuff you like, and while the music is playing you can also see the cover art, the length of the song, and where you are in the song. If you then drag open the menu, you can download the song, share it with others, or add it to your playlist.

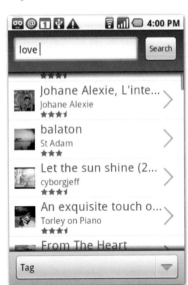

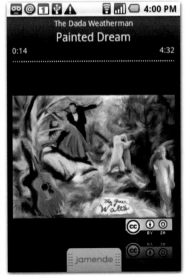

# Best Media Syncing App

## doubleTwist

**Free**
**doubleTwist Corporation**

One of the best software applications for Android isn't even technically an Android app. That is, it's designed for use with your Android phone, but you won't find it in the Market, because it's actually a desktop application for your Mac or PC. doubleTwist helps you buy and sync music from Amazon's MP3 store, iTunes, and any other music, video, or photo files that live on your desktop. It will even convert videos to the right format to watch on your device. Just drag and drop to take all your media with you.

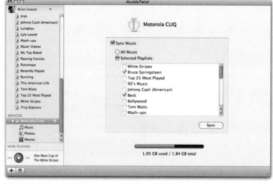

**IN SYNC:** Sync playlists from your iTunes library (as well as videos or photos) by dragging and dropping or just selecting the playlists you want to transfer. Your phone won't play DRM-protected songs from the iTunes Store, but most labels now offer DRM-free music on iTunes.

**MEDIA:** doubleTwist makes it easy to buy music from Amazon's MP3 store and sync it straight to your device. Just search by artist, album, or song to find what you're looking for. After connecting to your Amazon account through a browser, you can buy and download tunes right into the app.

# Salling Media Sync

**Free Lite / $22 Full version**
**Version:**
**Salling Software**

Salling Media Sync offers another option for syncing the iTunes library on your Mac or PC with your Android phone. Like doubleTwist, it's a desktop app, so you won't find it in the Market, but its functionality is so specific to your phone that we think it should count as an Android app. The paid version syncs faster, but unless you have a huge library and tons of storage space on your phone, you'll probably find that the free version transfers quickly enough.

**PODCASTS TO GO:** If you subscribe to podcasts and want to keep them up to date on your phone, Salling makes the sync easy for you. Just specify the shows and number of episodes, and the app does the rest. It even tells you when there are new episodes that haven't updated on your phone yet.

**KING OF ALL MEDIA:** Keep all your music, podcasts, and photos (though not video) synced in one place, though you'll want to keep an eye on how much space it's all taking up on your phone. Note that Salling doesn't bother transferring DRM-protected files that won't play on your device.

143

# Best Podcast Player

## Listen
Free
Version: 1.0.3.3
Google

If you have a standing engagement with audio programs online, there's no need to hunt around for new episodes or launch them from a link in an RSS reader. Let Google's Listen podcast manager find, organize, and stream all of your favorites in one place. Search for new programs, subscribe to channels, and download fresh shows as they're available. When you get behind on episodes, create a queue to remind you of the stuff you want to catch up on when you have some downtime.

**PODCAST PLAYER:** Listen makes it easy to find new podcasts and new episodes of your favorite shows. Subscribe to a channel, or just download the episode you want. When you're ready to listen, the app launches its own native media player so you can keep all your podcasts in one place, without having to open up your default media player.

**ALL TOGETHER NOW:** All of your subscriptions are stored together and kept separate from the rest of your media, which tends to be less time sensitive and has different organizational requirements. If you want to see what else is new while you're listening, you can access the rest of the app while an episode is playing.

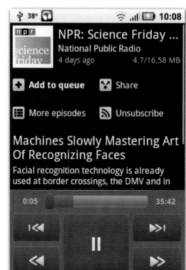

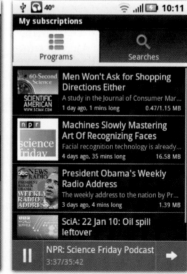

# BeyondPod
**Free trial / $6.99 Full version**
**Version: 2.1.4**
**Beyond Pod Team**

Though designed primarily for podcasts, BeyondPod is a full-featured RSS reader that pulls together a variety of media. In addition to listening to audio podcasts, you can view comics, subscribe to YouTube videos, and even get plain old text feeds with Google Reader integration. However, if you use another feed reader on your phone, the app starts to feel a little bloated, and even all its many features aren't as impressive as they could be (having no embedded player for YouTube feels clunky). All this makes the price (after a free seven-day trial) seem excessive.

**ORGANIZED FEEDS:** BeyondPod has a slick and attractive interface, organizing all of your feeds by category and offering a variety of views into the information and episodes for your shows. Group your feeds by content, or assign tags to make searching and discovering your shows easier.

**MANAGER WITHOUT A PLAYER:** Even with all the features offered by BeyondPod, it falls short on the main selling point you're looking for in a podcast manager: the playing of podcasts. That's because listening to a podcast requires you to pause and open the phone's default music player. This inability to play a podcast locally disrupts the media experience in what is otherwise a smooth app.

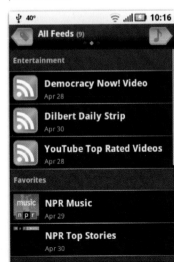

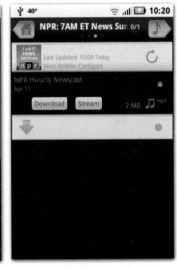

145

# Best Voice Recording App

## Recordoid Dictaphone

**Free Lite / $1.99 Full version**
**Version: 2.0.0**
**somyac**

With your podcast manager in place, you're ready to organize and consume audio created by others. But what if you want to actually create your own audio? Whether you're just capturing and organizing ideas with quick voice notes, creating a new ringtone, or launching your own podcast, Recordoid Dictaphone offers all the features you'll need to record, save, and send audio from your Android phone. It does it all in style too, with a flashy retro interface.

**OLD-SCHOOL INTERFACE:** With its retro interface taking up the entire screen, Recordoid Dictaphone makes your phone look like an old-fashioned dedicated voice recorder. The buttons respond with a satisfying click (you can disable the sound if you prefer), and the tape turns as the app is recording.

**AUDIO OPTIONS:** After recording, your audio clips are organized in one convenient list, from which you can play them, delete them, add text notes, or send them via email or text message (or in many other ways if you have Pixelpipe installed). You also have the option of saving location information on a map, just in case you need to remember exactly where you were when inspiration struck.

Entertainment

# Voice Recorder

**Free**
**Version: 1.9.7**
**Mamoru Tokashiki**

Voice Recorder offers most of the features of Recordoid Dictaphone (though no location information), but with a more stripped-down, utilitarian interface. Just hit Record and start talking. Give your recording a title and save it to your SD card. One advantage over Recordroid is the ability to schedule when you want recording to start by setting a timer. This could be useful for clandestine captures, but I can't think of many other virtuous uses.

**JUST PRESS RECORD:** The basic interface offers all you really need in a voice recorder, unless you require something really flashy. The Record button toggles to Stop while you're recording, and a list of your previous recordings is displayed beneath the button. The timer up top shows you how long you've been talking. That's about it!

**AUDIO OPTIONS:** Select a recording from your list to see your available options, which are essentially the same as in Recordoid Dictaphone. You can play the recording, send it by email or text message (or in many other ways if you have Pixelpipe installed), set it as your ringtone, edit the title, or delete the recording altogether.

# Best App for Media Sharing

## Pixelpipe
**Free Lite / $.99 Pro version**
**Version: 2.0.1**
**Pixelpipe**

You've recorded audio on your phone, or taken a picture or video. Where do you want it to go now? Most media apps offer a Share option, which sends by email or text message by default. Pixelpipe goes many steps further, connecting you with over 110 supported social networking services that should include just about anything you might use to connect with others. This allows you to go way beyond updating your status—you can turn your Android phone into a platform for blogging, podcasting, sharing photos and videos, or whatever else you need to become a mobile multimedia broadcaster.

**WHERE TO?:** After you've got that perfect snapshot, video capture, or podcast episode, connect with the social networking services you already use to get it online. Pixelpipe also adds itself as an option to the default Share or Send dialog in your camera, voice, and video recording apps. Note that audio and video options are available in the Pro version only, but they're well worth the extra buck.

**MO' MOBLOGGING OPTIONS:** Pixelpipe connects with almost any social networking service you can think of. Select your media and add a title or note, or toggle between Status and Blog interfaces to send a new text-only post. Add routing tags such as @facebook, @wordpress, @flickr, or @twitter to choose which services you want to update.

# Best App for Live Video Broadcasting

## Qik

**Free**
**Version: 0.1.60**
**Qik, Inc.**

While Pixelpipe lets you broadcast completed media pretty much anywhere you can think of, only Qik lets you stream *live* video directly from your Android phone to the Internet, where the world can watch in real time. Give your viewers your personal URL and tell them when you plan to start recording. When your show ends, keep your video archived for later viewing, or share it with your friends through social networks such as Facebook, Twitter, and YouTube.

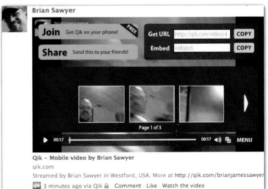

**MAKE SURE YOU'RE CONNECTED:** Get online and share your experience with the world as it happens. Qik works great for sharing precious family moments, and it's perfect for sneaking a colleague into that conference session he couldn't attend in person.

**REPEAT BROADCAST:** Did someone miss your live show? No worries. Keep everybody in the loop by sharing your broadcast with any or all of your social networking services. Send it to Twitter, link to it with a tweet, or embed it on your personal Facebook profile or as a post to a friend's wall.

149

# Best Camera App

## Snap Photo Pro
**$.99**
**Version: 1.5.7**
**Bratag**

The camera that comes by default on your Android phone is serviceable, but it doesn't do much more than point and shoot. When you replace it with Snap Photo Pro, you get a world of new features. Set the timer so you can get into your own shot, take multiple shots in succession, control for stability, and edit snapshots with filters, brightness/contrast settings, and more. Though the resolution is dictated by your hardware, your camera software doesn't need to be.

**PHOTO OPTIONS:** You have plenty of options to choose from. From left to right in the toolbar, you can adjust zoom scaling, white balance, night mode, timer duration, autofocus settings, default image size, multi-shot mode, and stability. You can even add clip-art props to your frame.

**AFTER EFFECTS:** Your options don't end once you've captured your subject. After saving the image, you can adjust levels (as shown here), add a border, crop, and more. This gives you as much editing power as you need for a camera app; for more, open your photo in PicSay.

# Best Photo Editing App

## PicSay

**Free / €1.99 Pro version**
**Version: 1.3.0.2**
**Shinycore 0.1.60**

Your photo isn't done when you cap-ture it and save it to your phone—at least it doesn't have to be. Whether you want to adjust color, contrast, and exposure to make the image look more professional, or you just want to have a little fun by adding text, graph-ics, distortion, and crazy effects, PicSay is a powerful photo editor for your Android phone. The interface itself is easy and fun to use, offering plenty of possibilities for turning your photos into works of art (high or low).

**FIX IT IN POST:** Clean up your photos for your photo blog, or create comic-book versions of family members to send via email or to the social network of your choice (using an add-on such as Pixelpipe).

**IN THE SPOTLIGHT:** Adding props, effects, titles, and other elements is easy and fun. The free version of PicSay comes with a pretty good selection of props and effects, but to really mix it up, go ahead and spring for the Pro version.

# Best Games

Ready for some real fun? In addition to the utility of its more "serious" applications, the Android operating system has quickly become a serious gaming platform, offering a wide selection of quality games in any genre you can think of. This chapter showcases the most addictive time-wasters available in the Android market.

Warm up with simple games to test the **speed of your thumbs,** and move on to fast-paced **matching** games with **balls**, **jewels**, and **tiles**. Volley back and forth with basement favorites like **air hockey** and **ping pong**. Play **multiplayer marbles** with online friends, or roll a marble through a **labyrinth**.

Race to victory or to the death with highly graphical **3D racing** games that take advantage of your phone's built-in accelerometer to steer **cars**, **light cycles**, and **futuristic hovercrafts**. And of course, get behind your guns in the best **first-person shooter**.

If you're in a retro mood, go back in time with a **Nintendo emulator**, classic **tower defense** scenarios, and **role-playing** games. Finally, challenge your **mental ability** with games that require strategy or smarts, from **cards** and **board** games to **word** games and brain testers. And then? Get back to work.

# Best Whack-a-Mole Game

## Poke A Mole

**Free**
**Version: 1.0.3**
**Software Industrial Co., LTD**

Take out your frustration on smug bur-rowing rodents with this virtual take on traditional carnival whack-a-mole. Just give 'em a whack as they pop up out of their holes to wipe those smiles off their annoying little faces. Great for kids or any adult with a pest-control problem in their own backyard. With a little practice playing this app, perhaps Carl Spackler would have finally gotten that darned gopher in *Caddyshack*.

**MOUNTAINS AND MOLEHILLS:** Three levels of difficulty let you adjust the number of holes on the screen to 9, 16, or 25. The more holes, the more moles, so you'll need to be a little more alert and quick with your fingers.

**THUMB THUMPER:** The easiest way to thump these critters as they spring from their holes is to cradle the phone in your palm and use your thumb as a weapon. If you find yourself in a slump at work, going a few rounds against these little pests is a great way to jumpstart your alertness and get your neurons firing a little more quickly.

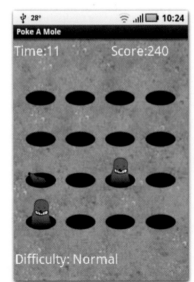

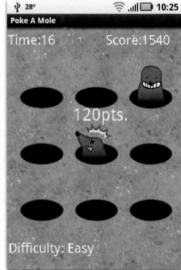

# Best Soccer Juggling Game

## Keepy Uppy
**Free / £0.59 Pro version**
**Version: 3.2**
**BrightAI**

Another test for the alacrity of your thumbs, Keepy Uppy is a simple soccer juggling game that's fun for kids and an easy way for adults to keep alert while passing idle moments. All you have to do is control the ball and keep it in the air. The free version now includes target mode and a worldwide leaderboard (previously available only in the Pro version), which lets you see how your soccer skillz stack up against the rest of the world.

**BALLS IN THE AIR:** Maybe you can juggle with your feet, but have you ever tried doing it with your thumbs? Choose Free mode to score based on the number of touches before the ball hits the ground, or Target mode to get points for hitting numbers on the screen. The numbers pop up, and count down from 5 to 1 before disappearing.

**LEADERBOARD:** Keepy Uppy stores local high scores for your device, but if you want to see how other people are doing, check out the worldwide leaderboard. Can you imagine touching the ball over 13,000 times before letting it drop? That takes some skill—and a lot of free time on your hands. The ads are fairly unobtrusive, but if you'd rather get rid of them, buy the Pro version for less than a British pound.

# Best Ball-Matching Game

## Bonsai Blast

**Free Lite / $4.99 Pro version**
**Version: 1.2**
**Glu Mobile**

Shoot colored balls at a line of other colored balls as they march toward the yin/yang at the end of their path. Matching three or more balls in a row destroys all balls in that color string and sets up future matches. When the first ball in the line makes it to the end, the whole line speeds down the hole that opens up and you've lost the level. But make enough matches to clear the board, and you're on to one of the many other levels in the game.

**BONSAI ADVENTURE:** I don't even know how many levels this game has, but it's plenty to keep you going for a good long time. I've made it through the 24 levels of the Morning section and 11 of the Afternoon levels of Adventure mode (each section is locked until you beat the previous section), and I still have Evening and 24 other levels waiting for me in Survival mode.

**HAVE A BLAST:** After some success with matching balls, you get to fire special balls that explode whatever they hit (or the balls around what they hit in some cases), without having to match anything. These special balls come in handy as a hard-to-match ball gets closer and closer to its destination. If you can get a clear shot, hitting the treasure chest gets you bonus points.

# Best Gem-Swapping Game

## Jewellust
**Free Lite / $2.99 Full version**
**Version: 2.0.7**
**Smartpix Games**

If you've ever played Bejeweled, you'll find Jewellust a familiar addition to your handheld game library. Swap adjacent jewels to line up three or more of the same color, at which point all of the like-colored gems connected in the line disappear and cause the gems they support to drop. The Free version will certainly keep you occupied for a while, but if you need more variety, the Full version features 30 levels and a Survival mode.

**PRECIOUS GEMS:** Connect the matching jewels to watch them collapse together and cause the rest of the column or row to fall. If you're stuck and don't make a move for a few seconds, you'll get a little hint, in the form of arrows that suggest which gems could be swapped to form a match.

## Bejeweled
**$4.99**
**Version: 5.38.56**
**EA Mobile**

Bejeweled is the original and classic gem-swapping game, selling millions of copies on a variety of platforms since its birth as a browser-based game in 2001. But for those of us who are more conscious of cost than pedigree in a game, Jewellust gets the job done well enough for free (or three bucks for all the options). So the game that started it all is reduced to honorable mention status, mainly for its high price and lack of a free trial.

# Best Tile-Matching Game

## Mahjong

**Free**
**Version: 1.0.4**
**Magma Mobile**

Based on the classic Chinese game for four players, Mahjong solitaire is a tile-matching game that begins with a set of 144 tiles arranged in a variety of layouts. Tiles that you can move left or right without disturbing other tiles are considered "exposed." Your task is to find pairs of identical exposed tiles (Season tiles are also considered matches). Selecting a pair removes the tiles from the layout. The game ends when the layout is empty, when no exposed pairs remain, or when your patience runs out.

**TAKE IT BACK:** Mahjong involves strategy far beyond just finding matches. The goal for each move is to remove pairs in an order that will open up possibilities for other matches. So even if you find a match, it might not be the *best* possible move and might actually close up the board for future moves. If you regret a match, you can undo a move by pressing the yellow arrow in the lower-right. You get three chances to undo.

**TAKE A HINT:** If you find yourself struggling or completely stumped, press the lightbulb in the lower-left corner of the screen. You'll be asked if you want to take a hint, which the game offers by highlighting an exposed match in red. The next move is up to you. You're allowed three hints; after that, you're on your own.

# Best Volley Game

## Air Hockey

**Free Demo / $.99 Full version**
**Version: 1.1.3**
**JJCgames**

Put your game playing on ice with this virtual simulation of the air hockey table at your local arcade. As with the "real" game, the first to score seven goals wins. The free demo has a single skill level, but the full version keeps track of your record and advances to four different levels as you improve. Your automated opponent gets tougher at higher skill levels, and the puck speed increases.

**UNDER MY THUMB:** Keeping your thumb on the virtual mallet can be a little tricky because there's a short lag as the mallet trails behind where you press; still, it's close enough to keep things interesting and fun. Keep track of your score by looking in the lower-left corner (I'm up 3-1 in this shot). Your virtual opponent gets a counter to read too, just to complete the illusion of reality.

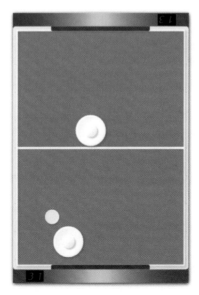

## Zen Table Tennis

**Free Lite / $4.99 Pro version**
**Version: 1.0.3**
**RESETgame**

This is just ping pong for thumbs. The lite version displays ads and plays up to a two-point advantage; the full version offers complete 11-point games.

159

# Best Digging Game

## Gem Miner

**Free**
**Version: 1.0.5**
**Psym Mobile**

Dig deep into the earth to discover coal, ores, gems, fossils, and other underground treasures to make you rich. Fill your pack and return to the surface before you run out of stamina; you can then exchange your finds for cash to buy upgrades to your tools, ladders for climbing, support beams to keep tunnels from caving in, and more. Be careful not to fall down a mine shaft, run out of time, or get crushed by falling rocks, and you'll make your fortune in the mines.

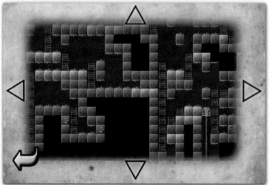

**DIG IT:** Hammer away in the mine shaft to find your rewards buried within the rocks. Gray stones are impervious to your pickaxe, and will fall and crush you if you don't place a support under them quickly enough. And always make sure you have enough ladders to make it back to the surface.

**TREASURE MAP:** It's dark down there, so your view is limited to a small radius. To get an idea of where you are, pull up the map, which shows you how to get back out. The map shows only what you've discovered—the black areas remain a mystery.

# Best Minesweeper Game

## aiMinesweeper

**Free**
**Version: 2.0.3**
**ArtfulBits Inc.**

The classic minesweeper game gets a flashy facelift in this version for Android. The board starts with completely filled-in boxes hiding numbers and mines beneath them, which are revealed when you tap a box with your finger. The numbers indicate how many mines border that particular box (touching the left, right, top, bottom, or one of the four corners), helping you figure out which spaces to avoid.

**BOOM:** Select a box on the screen by pressing it with your finger to reveal what lies beneath. Assuming you don't hit a mine (which ends the game and reveals where the rest of the mines were located), the surrounding bomb-free spaces will clear and leave the numbers that will guide you on future moves. To win, clear the board of all spaces except the mines.

**SKIN IT:** Change your level to Intermediate or Expert to expand the board (notice the arrows to scroll for more screen). Additional (and free) skins are also available in the Market to customize the look and feel of your board. This White Snow skin features a pleasant white theme with large cells that are easy to press, making it less likely that you'll accidentally select a neighboring mine.

# Best Trapping Game

## Trap!
**Free**
**Version: 1.00**
**Matt Wachowski**

Take ownership of increasing swaths of real estate on your phone's screen by carefully boxing up sections and avoiding the bouncing balls. You create these boxes by drawing lines on the screen, "capturing" the space inside them. When you create a box around a ball, you "trap" it and earn extra points. Capture more than 70% of the screen to win and progress to the next level. You can also trap a variety of special balls to give you extra life, speed, and other bonuses.

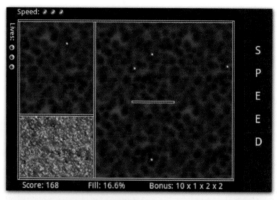

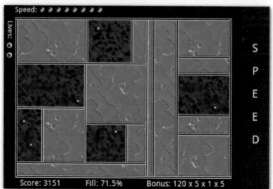

**ALL BOXED IN:** Start drawing a line by sliding your finger a small distance, either horizontally or vertically. If a moving ball hits your line before it reaches the edges, the line disappears and you lose a life. Create boxes to capture screen area or trap balls in a confined area.

**NEED FOR SPEED:** Tap the blue bar labeled SPEED on the right side to cause your next line to zip across the screen almost instantly. These moves are limited (check the top of the screen to see how many you have left), but you can earn more by capturing speed balls in your boxes.

# Best Pinball Game

## Pinball

Free
Version: 1.1.7
Magma Mobile

Shake the table all you want and never tilt with this Android-based pinball game. It doesn't use your phone's accelerometer to allow you to influence the motion of the ball, but given how easy it is to rock your phone while you're pressing the flippers, perhaps that's actually a feature. You have the option to control flippers with the touchscreen or with customizable button presses (for phones with a physical keyboard).

**PINBALL WIZARD:** Capture the feel of traditional pinball with boards reminiscent of the big arcade machines. Begin by launching your ball with the spring on the right (it doesn't seem like you can adjust the force, so just press with your finger) and watch the targets ding. Use your flippers to keep the ball up and out of the gutters.

**FANCY FLIPPERS:** The Pinball app offers five different tables to choose from, including a 60s theme (shown on the left), Android land (shown below), Invaders (in the style of Space Invaders), Soccer, and Underwater. So score a goal, zap an alien, or take aim at a robot. It's all in good fun.

# Best Labyrinth Game

## Kumpa
**Free**
**Version: 1.1.0**
**greenrobot**

You know those games where you have to use gravity and the tilting of the board to navigate a marble through the maze? Well, take away the physical board and add a story, some adventure, and a few other fun features and you have Kumpa, an adventure game that takes you through the labyrinths of ancient Incan temples. Like the traditional game, Kumpa relies on gravity (via your phone's accelerometer) to move the ball. Tilt your phone to move through the maze, activating energy fields to teleport to other temples.

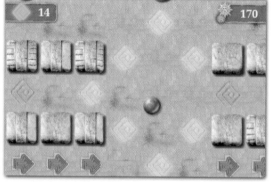

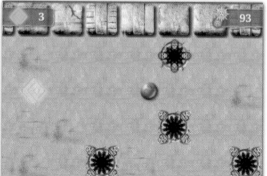

**ENERGY FIELDS:** The object of the game is to activate (turn blue) all of the energy fields on the level, which enables you to teleport on to the next level (each level is locked until you complete the previous one). Each level is timed; the time you have left is shown in the upper-right corner.

**DEATH TRAPS:** As you make your way through the maze, beware of death traps (the black and red holes shown in the screenshot on the left), slick metallic fluids, cracks in the floor, and other obstacles. These were put in place by the Incan gods to foil your attempts to navigate the temples.

# Best Marbles Game

## Cestos Full

**Free**
**Version: 1.34**
**Chicken Brick Studios**

Cestos allows you to take your marbles from the playground to your phone, where you can play with your friends in real time. This multiplayer marbles game lets you find your friends or meet new competitors in the lobby. Chat and socialize while you whack each other's marbles into pits, over mines, or into other obstacles. To win, be the last player with at least one marble remaining on the map. Successes unlock new customizations for your marbles' avatars.

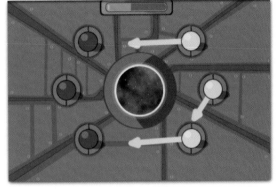

**FUNNIES:** Touch a marble with your finger and drag away from it to create an arrow in the direction you want to send your marble. The length of the arrow defines how far the marble will go. Set up all of your marbles in this way and when you're ready for action, hit the scroll bar.

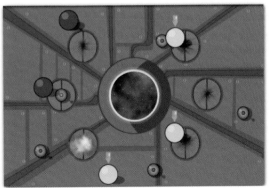

**LOSE YOUR MARBLES:** Avoid the pits while trying to send your opponent's marbles down them. Mines won't immediately destroy your marbles, but you'll lose one if it hits enough mines. If you lose, demand a rematch to challenge your friend or foe to another one.

165

# Best Car Racing Game

## Raging Thunder
**Free Lite / €3.00 Full version**
**Version: 1.0.7**
**Polarbit AB**

One of the most popular car games ever for mobile phones (especially on the iPhone), Raging Thunder is now available in the Android Market. Movement in this realistic 3D course is controlled by the accelerometer in your phone. Just hold it like a steering wheel and tilt right or left to turn. Pitch the phone forward to speed up and pull it back to slow down. While the Lite version offers only one playable level and one choice of car, the Full version gives you other gameplay car choices.

**BURN RUBBER:** The different race modes offered in the Full version of the app allow you to race against time, CPU, or up to three friends . Choose your car, select your track, get your friends behind the wheel, and start your engines for the virtual ride of your life.

**UP TO SPEED:** Though you'll get the hang of steering with practice, it's a little tougher to catch up with the CPU-controlled competitors without tilting the phone so far forward you can't see the screen. After a few practice runs, you'll perfect your racing technique.

Games

# Best Powerboat Racing Game

## Wave Blazer

**Free Lite / €3.00 Full version**
**Version: 1.0.4**
**Polarbit AB**

Like Raging Thunder (also by Polarbit), Wave Blazer uses your phone's accelerometer to control your movement. Here, it makes it feel like your boat is really speeding across the rich aquatic landscape, whether it's in a spectacular natural setting or a fetid city sewer. The Full version offers a choice of boats (the Lite version has only one) and three playing modes to choose from: Grand Prix, Time Trials, and Arcade (the Lite has only Arcade). The Lite version times out quickly, so if you're having fun, pay a few Euro for the real thing.

**I'M ON A BOAT:** You really feel like you're speeding through the waterways when you steer your boat through the course. Tilt your phone left or right to turn, tip forward to speed up, and pull back to slow down. Watch out for the hazards, or you'll find yourself floating in a corner.

**WAKEY WAKEY:** Leave other boats in your wake when you make your turns. Hit ramps head on to land on course. If you find yourself off course and out of control, hitting the Auto Pilot button will give you a few seconds to get your boat back on track.

167

# Best Light-Racing Game

## Light Racer 3D
**Free Basic / $2.49 Full version**
**Version: 1.2e**
**Battery Powered Games, LLC**

Take yourself into the futuristic Tron-like environment of light-trailing motorcycles racing to the death in a graphically rich 3D world. Rather than racing to a finish line, the object is to force your opponent to crash into the blue stream of light in your wake (which acts like a wall) and avoid crashing into the yellow stream of light in your opponent's wake.

MASTER CONTROL PROGRAM : The graphics in this game are great, and the 3D point of view puts you in the middle of the action for added excitement. But that perspective comes with a price: it's much harder to know the whereabouts of your opponent (and his trail) without the broader birds-eye view of the original 2D Light Racer.

 **HONORABLE MENTION**

## Light Racer
**Free**
**Version: 2.0f**
**Battery Powered Games LLC**

If you don't need the graphics of the 3D version, the original 2D version of Light Racer lets you see the whole board and action from a much clearer vantage point.

Games

# Best First-Person Shooter Game

## ToonWarz

**Free Demo / €3.00 Full version**
**Version: 1.0.7**
**Polarbit AB**

These days, no gaming platform is complete without a good first-person shooter, and ToonWarz is the best out there for Android. Go on a single-player mission by yourself, or play real-time death matches with your friends (Full version only). You can move around by tilting your phone (relying on the built-in accelerometer) or sliding the on-screen controls with your fingers. ToonWarz supports multi-touch on Android 2.0 devices, but you may prefer the precision of a physical keyboard or a trackpad.

**ON A MISSION:** The Full version offers three skill levels and four missions for a variety of playing scenarios. There's not much action in the demo and it times out pretty quickly, so if you like the feel of the game you'll want to get the Full version for serious playing.

**FIRE AT WILL:** With the screen controls, you have all your options at the touch of a finger. Walk around by pressing and dragging the button on the left, look around with the button on the right, select your weapon by pressing the weapon icon, and fire away by pressing the crosshairs.

# Best Tower Defense Game

## Robo Defense
**Free trial / $2.99 Full version**
**Version: 1.2.0**
**Lupis Labs Software**

If you prefer to take your time and focus more on strategy than the speed of your reflexes, you'll love tower defense games. The Market has more than a few to choose from, but the most popular is Robo Defense. As with all games in the genre, the goal is to stop invaders by building towers to shoot at them as they pass. For each move, purchase and place your towers, upgrade them, move them to more strategic locations, and then brace yourself for the attack.

**LINE OF FIRE:** Use your money wisely to purchase a few towers to add to your map (click on the prices at the bottom of the screen for details on each tower). Drag them with your finger to a strategic location, and then begin the first wave of attack. After that, it's out of your hands, as your tower takes over the actual shooting.

**TOWER DEFENSE:** The more money you earn by destroying enemies, the more and better towers (and stronger and faster weapons) you can afford. The free version includes all tower options and 11 difficulty levels, but only one map. Upgrade to the Full version for much more variety.

# Retro Defense

**Free Lite / $4.99 Full version**
**Version: 1.2.3**
**Larva Labs Ltd.**

Retro Defense is another great tower defense game—so great that it's hard to relegate it to honorable mention status. Though the classic look and more realistic graphics likely make Robo Defense more popular, I prefer the simpler look, feel, and sound of Retro Defense. Like other tower defense games, you buy and build your defenses to prepare for an enemy attack. Place your towers strategically (you'll have to use your imagination a bit, as 2D tower isn't a "tower" per se) and wait for the neon invaders.

**BEST DEFENSE:** After you select a tower for purchase, drag it with your finger to a cell on the grid (the green area in the middle is the path the invaders take through the map). When you're satisfied, select Next Wave to trigger the next pass of invaders to come charging down the screen. The Lite version of the game offers just one level, but the full version includes 24.

**TOWER MARKET:** Between waves, you can purchase new towers, upgrade existing towers, or move your towers to more strategic locations, based on the results of the previous wave. Both free and paid versions of the game include 12 upgradeable tower types, 6 invader types, and 3 types of bonus tower.

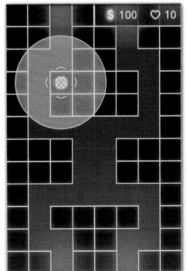

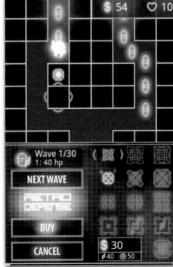

# Best Nintendo Emulator

## Nesoid
**Free Lite / $3.49 Full version**
**Version: 1.7**
**yongzh**

Feeling nostalgic for those old 8-bit games, or just in the mood to go retro? Nesoid isn't a game, but rather a platform on your Android phone for playing the old NES games you used to love. And there are plenty of public domain and freeware NES console games out there for you to find. Search for a ROM (a read-only memory file from the original cartridge) online by opening a browser window from the app. Then, download it to your phone and load it up in Nesoid to get playing!

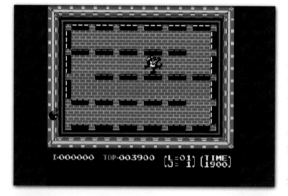

**DOWNLOAD:** Choosing Search ROM from within Nesoid opens your browser to Rom Find (*romfind.com*). You can also go to any URL that hosts files, like PDRoms (*pdroms.de/files/NES*), which carries public domain ROMs such as Bombsweeper (*pdroms.de/files/1247*), shown here.

**LOAD AND PLAY:** After downloading and saving a ROM to your phone, your system will recognize it and launch Nesoid, or you can browse to games like Sack of Flour (*pdroms.de/files/1259*) from within the app. The Lite version will get you far, but buying the full version enables you to load game states.

# Best Role-Playing Game

## Dungeon Quest
**Free 20 gems, more at various prices**
Version: 1.82.AGI.000
Moblyng

Another throwback that might satisfy a nostalgic urge, Dungeon Quest simulates the style of play found in the old Dungeons and Dragons game. Choose your character and avatar, pick your weapons, select a mission, and go on a quest in this fantasy role-playing game. Win fights or accomplish feats to gain the strength and experience needed to advance to the next level. Play against your phone or challenge your friends, either on their phones or through Facebook.

**ARM YOURSELF:** "Gems" are an in-game currency you can spend on health upgrades, weapons, and other items. The free version of the game comes with 20 gems; if you want more gems for your character, you can buy various packages at around 10 cents a gem (50 gems for $4.99, 100 gems for $9.99, 200 gems for $19.99, and so on).

**WHAT'S YOUR DAMAGE?:** To gain experience, challenge another character to a fight. Just challenge them and press FIGHT to instantly see the outcome of your duel. Results will be based on your relative strengths, health, and weapons.

# Best Texas Hold 'Em Game

## Red Poker Club

**Free**
**Version: 2.0.1**
**Somobi**

Play the style of poker that's become a favorite with professional gamblers, celebrity players, and sports entertainment outlets in this flashy, multiplayer version of Texas Hold 'Em. You get $5,000 in chips daily (virtual, not the real thing!). Just log in, find yourself a table, and start gambling with other players. It takes a little time to get comfortable with the mechanics of how the game works, but that could also be said of Texas Hold 'Em itself.

**DEAL ME IN:** This game isn't for wallflowers, as there's no option to just play against your phone. Once you have your avatar set up, log in to find a virtual table with other real people playing on their own phones. Create a buddy list of regulars, or get to know the community through the game's Facebook fan page.

**HOW TO PLAY:** Start with two cards in your hand and five community cards. Bet on what's in your hand before any community cards are shown (this stage is known as "the blind"), then again when the first three are shown ("the flop"), and so on. The best five-card poker hand wins.

# Best Solitaire Game

## Fun Towers

**Free**
Version: 1.4
blatter.com

No gaming platform is complete without a solid solitaire app. Fun Towers is a variation on the standard solitaire we've all played to death on our computers. Instead of creating stacks of suits above the dealt hand, you pull cards from the layout back into your stack. The basic concept is the same: match cards one value apart from each other to reveal hidden cards beneath them. You have to hurry, though, because you get only a limited amount of time before the game ends.

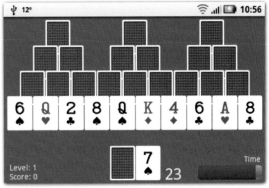

**THE DEAL:** Press a card with a value one higher or one lower than the card revealed next to the stack at the bottom of the screen. This will send the match to your stack and turn over the card beneath it. If you don't have any moves with the cards in front of you, press the stack to reveal a new card.

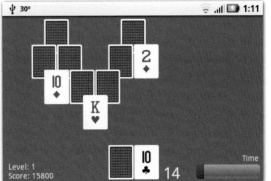

**TIME RUNNING OUT:** The red bar in the lower-right corner shows your time ticking down, but it doesn't tell you exactly how many seconds you have to complete the game. But as a special service to readers of this book, we can say that you get two minutes total.

175

# Best Chess and Checkers Games

## Chess and Checkers for Android

There are plenty of apps in the Market for the classic games of chess and checkers, but these selections should save you some valuable searching time. With simple graphics and few features, Aart Bik has created two games that give you everything you need for playing chess and checkers on your Android phone. No frills here, but it's solid and stable, and most fans of the games would prefer functionality over flashy pieces and boards any day. Both games offer play at various levels, a record of moves, and undo up to eight plays.

## Chess for Android
**Free**
**Version: 2.1.1**
**Aart Bik**

THE GAME OF KINGS: The Chess app takes touchscreen, trackball, or keyboard input. Select a move and valid possibilities are highlighted, as is your last played move.

## Checkers for Android
**Free**
**Version: 2.1.1**
**Aart Bik**

SMOKE BEFORE FIRE: Checkers shares the features of Chess, allowing touchscreen or trackball input, highlighting possible moves, and the option for mandatory or optional captures.

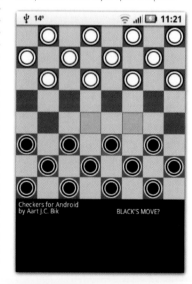

Games

# Best Sudoku Game

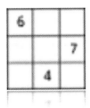

## Sudoku Free

**Free / $1.99 Premium version**
**Version: 8.1.5**
**genina.com**

There's no shortage of sudoku games in the Market, but weeding through them all to find the best can really drain your game-playing time. This version from genina.com has the most intuitive and accessible interface, allowing input from touchscreen, trackball, or keyboard. It also features a history record, the ability to upload results to track your progress on the Internet, and competitions with other players in the community.

**BASICS AND FEATURES:** To play, fill in the grid with numbers such that every row, column, and 3 x 3 box contains every digit from 1 to 9. When you press a box in the grid (or select it with your keypad or trackball), you see all the number options for that space. Just select the number to fill in the square.

**HINTS AND SOLUTIONS:** Each of the four difficulty levels offers hints upon request and the ability to undo or redo a move. At any time, you can choose to validate the puzzle to see whether what you have so far is correct. If you find yourself stuck and ready to give up, just ask for the solution. The Premium version is the same as the free version, but without the ads.

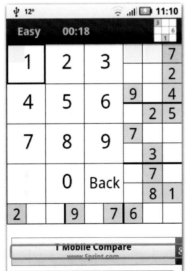

# Best Word-Search Game

## WordUp!

**Free / $2.99 Full version**
**Version: 1.2.3**
**Anthrological**

Word freaks have a few quality options for games that look and feel like Boggle, but WordUp! gets everything just right. Presented with a grid of letters (choose between 3×3, 4×4, or 5×5), find as many words as you can in the jumble by connecting letters horizontally, vertically, or diagonally. Set your minimum word length and time limit, and get solving. If you're stuck, rotate the board. Buying the upgrade disables ads but doesn't give you any additional features.

WORD SEARCH: Occasionally, the touchscreen is a little too sensitive when you're sliding your fingers across to make a word (selecting letters adjacent to the one you want), so it might be nice to have an option to select letters individually. Still, when it works (which is most of the time), not having to hit Enter sure does speed things up.

## Wixel

**Free Lite / $1.49 Full version**
**Version: 1.1h**
**Battery Powered Games, LLC**

Choose a 4×4 or 5×5 game board in a clean, attractive interface. See played words and track your statistics. The full version includes online play.

# Best Crossword Puzzle

## Crosswords
Free
Version: 0.9.9
Tea.ch

Addicted to crosswords? This app gives you a clean, simple interface to play the wealth of puzzles archived online in the popular Across Lite format used by electronic versions of many daily newspapers, including the *New York Times*. Load *.puz* files from your SD card or go to the app page at *crosswords.tea.ch* to find links to current and older puzzles online. No matter where you are, with this app you'll never run out of puzzles when you need your fix.

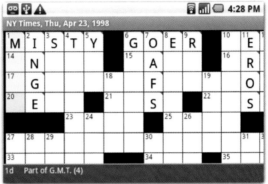

**PUZZLER:** The *New York Times* offers classic crossword puzzles like this one for free. Just navigate to the page from the Crossword Sources link at *crosswords.tea.ch* and select "Solve this puzzle in Across Lite" to download and start playing. You'll need to be a Premium *Times* subscriber to have access to today's puzzle.

**CROSSWORD CLUES:** Select a box to highlight the row or column and see the clue at the bottom of the screen (as shown above). Zoom out to see the entire board, or zoom in to focus on one area. You can also get hints by revealing a letter, a word, or the solution to the whole puzzle.

# Best Brain Workout Game

## Brain Genius Deluxe

**Free**
**Version: 1.16**
**Glu Mobile**

Give your brain a daily workout to keep yourself sharp, or really test yourself with deeper challenges in this game designed as a fun way to increase your mental performance. With 24 original touch and motion-controlled games, Brain Genius Deluxe trains your brain in observation, memory, calculation, and reasoning. Who says video games have to numb your brain? Even if that were true (and it's not), you can tell the doubters that this one is actually made to enhance your thinking power.

**MIND GAMES:** There's a variety of games to choose from, but you need to progress through each category in order (each question requires you to solve the previous one before it's unlocked). Progressing through levels increases your brain rating, and when your rating gets high enough, a few bonus games (Sudoku, Sliding Puzzle, CrossPix, and Jigsaw) unlock to challenge you even further.

**DAILY EXERCISE:** The game's animated professor, Dr. Labadini, can be a little patronizing with his unnecessary teasing, but sometimes the most frustrating coach can give you the best workouts. The professor strongly encourages you to test yourself every day, but if you can get through the snark, the exercises are actually worth trying out whenever *you* feel like it.

# Best Math Workout Game

## Maths Workout

**Free Lite / €1.49 Full version**
**Version: 1.59**
**Workout Games**

Another daily mental exercise game, Maths Workout tests your ability to solve math problems in your head and improves your mental arithmetic. See how well you can do basic addition or subtraction in your head, try for speed with multiplication and division challenges, play the Maths Blaster (kind of like Space Invaders, but you "shoot" math problems with correct answers), or compete in the online world challenge. The Brain Cruncher game and customizable wallpapers are available in the full version only.

**MENTAL ARITHMETIC:** Maths Workout tests your ability to do simple math in your head while progressing through a series of steps. Keep the first solution in your mind and apply the operation that follows to determine the final result. Each game starts off pretty easy, but more challenging levels are unlocked as you progress.

**LET'S REVIEW:** If you fail the exercise and you just want confirmation of your result, you have the chance to review all operations in the segment after you complete all the steps. When things start speeding up, you might be surprised how difficult it can be to complete even simple operations under pressure.

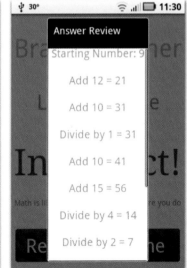

# Best Utility/Tool Apps

Your Android phone has the potential to be the **Swiss Army Knife** of mobile devices—with the right stuff, it can do just about anything you need. All you have to do is load it up with apps that transform your phone into **whatever you need it to be**.

For instance, when you travel, you might use your phone to track expenses and keep in touch with family. But if you want to wring the **highest perform-ance** out of your device, you'll also want apps that help you get the most out of your **battery**, **GPS**, **wireless**, and other features.

The utilities in this chapter help you do that and more, from enhancing the performance of your **battery** to discovering which apps are running and tak-ing up the most **space** and **memory**. Turn your phone into a **night light** or an **alarm clock**. The Android Market is full of useful utilities, and in the pages that follow we introduce you to some of the best. Read on to see how to get the most out of your Android-powered device.

# Best App for Creating Shortcuts

## Any Cut
**Free**
**Version: 1.2**
**Jeff Hamilton**

Out of the box, your Android device can create several kinds of shortcuts. Any Cut lets you create many more. Choose Activity from the menu, and you can map your actions, keystrokes, apps, folders, files, and more to a shortcut. For example, if there's a particular person you end up texting a lot, you can create an Any Cut Direct Text Message shortcut for that person and send her a text with one tap. To use Any Cut, press and hold on the home screen, select Shortcut, and choose Any Cut.

**MAP TO ANYTHING:** This app lets you map directly to a phone call, text message, activity, or other action. For example, by clicking Activity and then Wireless & Network Settings, you can create a shortcut to your WiFi settings, eliminating the need to install a separate WiFi management utility. Similarly, you can set other Activity shortcuts to take the place of various system management utilities.

**LIST OF EVERYTHING:** If you want to map it, chances are it's in the Activity list. I created a shortcut to send a text message to my teen daughter, and another that brings me to Amazon MP3, where I can see the top-selling songs on Amazon. Shortcuts can be placed on any home screen; you may want to dedicate one screen to all your shortcuts, and then launch activities from there.

Utilities/Tools

# dg QuickCut
**Free**
**Version: 1.2**
**Mike DG**

Why mess around with pushing a bunch of buttons or navigating through endless screens to get to the app or document you want? With dg QuickCut, you can create a shortcut that you activate with a key, or add shortcuts to the system notification bar or to one of your home screens. This app also includes toggles for wireless options, including GPS, WiFi, and Bluetooth.

**SHORTCUT OR DROPCUT:** dg QuickCut offers two types of quick access. Creating a shortcut puts an icon on any screen you want, whereas a dropcut appears in your system notification bar, so you can get to it from wherever you are. You can also create a quicklaunch keyboard shortcut, so if you find yourself constantly opening a certain app, map it to two keys on either side of your phone for quick access.

# BetterCut
**$1.99**
**Version: 2.0**
**Better Android**

This is an enhanced alternative to AnyCut that also lets you create home screen shortcuts. To create a shortcut with BetterCut, press and hold your finger down on the screen, tap shortcut, and then choose BetterCut. This simple process allows you to easily map all kinds of activities to a shortcut. BetterCut offers quick access to system settings, shortcuts to activities and phone calls, and more.

# Best App for Remote Terminal Access

## ConnectBot

**Free**
**Version: 1.5.5**
**Kenny Root and Jeffrey Sharkey**

Sometimes you need to communicate with a Unix, Linux, or Mac server over a terminal connection to perform system maintenance, check your mail, or run some other app. ConnectBot allows you to connect to servers over Telnet or SSH (Secure Shell), and can also open a local command-line prompt on your Android device. Once you've opened a session, just type your Unix commands and see the output on the 80-column screen that appears.

**CLEAN AND SIMPLE:** ConnectBot is nothing more than a terminal window that allows you to communicate with a remote or local shell. To connect, tap the menu button labeled "ssh" in the lower-left corner, and choose ssh, telnet, or local. If you're connecting to a remote server over SSH or Telnet, you'll have to log in with your password before you can run any commands..

**SIMPLE CAN BE HUGE:** Suppose you manage a website, and something crashes just as you're sitting down to a fancy dinner at the hip new restaurant in town. If you don't want to leave before your main course arrives, just fire up ConnectBot, restart your web server, and you're good to go. You can even poke around the server logs while you're in there, to make sure everything's running as it should.

# Best App for Terminal Access

## Android Terminal Emulator
Free
Version: 1.0.4
Jack Palevich

Lurking under the hood of your Android device is a Linux-based operating system. You can use Android all day without even thinking about it, but if you want to, you can peek beneath the surface by installing Android Terminal Emulator. This app opens up the command line, a sometimes cryptic interface to the deepest parts of Android. You use the command line to type commands into the shell. For example, "ls" lists the files in your current directory, and "cd" changes your current directory to somewhere else on the Android filesystem.

**KEY MAPPING:** In a regular terminal emulator you need to type a lot of keystrokes using the Control key, which isn't present on the Android keyboard. Android Terminal Emulator lets you use the scroll ball in combination with a keystroke to send Control sequences. This is especially useful when you use a text editor or other program that depends on the Control key.

**ARE YOU REALLY CONNECTED?:** Wondering why you can't reach a website even though you have a solid network connection? Fire up Android Terminal Emulator and use the "ping" command to see whether the site is really up. If you can't reach it, or if the times shown are very long (more than a few hundred milliseconds), try pinging another website. If the results come back quickly, then the first site is probably down temporarily.

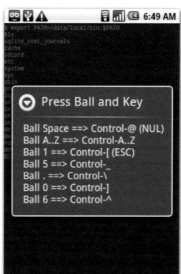

187

# Best App for Managing Your Apps

## aTrackDog

**Free**
**Version: 3.1.1**
**Sam Lu**

aTrackDog is a great app for tracking all the apps you have installed. Various settings allow you to view your apps by size or name, and you can see at a glance which ones need updating. You can view the size of each app as well as old and new version numbers. There's also a button to take you directly to your phone's application settings, where you can force quit, uninstall, or clear an app's cache. This app was invaluable in writing this book, as many of the apps covered here were updated multiple times in a little more than 2 months.

**COMPARE LISTS:** The Export App List menu item allows you to get a list of all your apps and version numbers and either send the list to yourself or save it on your SD card. You can send the list to friends and tell them which apps you like, or copy the contents to the clipboard and paste them into an email or an Evernote note.

**QUICK UPDATING:** To update your apps, select the option to Install from the Market. If you have a credit card tied to your Google Checkout, you can proceed quickly and update your free and paid apps. You can also uninstall the app or quit tracking the version. Tapping and holding an item will bring up more information, including the option to share with a friend.

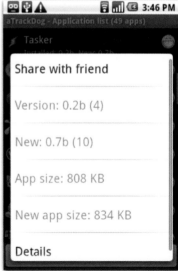

Utilities/Tools

# Advanced Task Killer

**Free / $4.99 Full version**
**Version: 1.7.0.34**
**ReChild**

Did you know that leaving an app does not necessarily mean the app stops running? Many apps stay open to gather information about a variety of things, including your GPS location, connection state, security status, and other items. Advanced Task Killer can stop those apps and free up some memory, while at the same time coaxing a few more hours out of your battery. Just shut down any unnecessary apps and run only the ones you absolutely need.

**IGNORE LIST:** To make sure you don't kill any apps that you really need, create an ignore list that will leave the specified apps unharmed. Use the settings to decide whether you want the app to start up when you power your phone on. Advanced Task Killer also lets you specify what to do when you tap or tap and hold on an app.

# Quick Uninstall

**Free**
**Version: 1.0.2**
**David Blackman**

You know how it happens. You load up your device with a bunch of cool apps, use them for the better part of a week, and then poof—you lose interest. With this simple tool, you can delete your "so last-week" apps quickly and efficiently. Just open it up to view a list of your installed apps. Tap the app in question, and you'll be prompted to uninstall the app or cancel, leaving it unharmed. This is a quick, easy way to get rid of a bunch of apps at once.

# Best App to Manage Power Usage

## Power Manager
**Free / $0.99 Full version**
**Version: 1.6.3**
**X-Phone Software, Inc.**

You've probably figured out by now that running all these apps, especially graphically rich games, can really suck the life out of your battery. Power Manager will help you extend battery life and manage the power usage of your phone. You can set up different profiles and quickly switch between them when you need to conserve your remaining power; for example, when your battery reaches 30% or less, you can set your phone to not synchronize with Google. This allows you to preserve your battery for phone calls and other high-priority things when you're running low.

**PROFILES:** Power Manager comes with several preloaded profiles that you can select from. Choosing one of the default profiles is a great option, but you'll likely want to create your own customized profiles for specific needs. You can also edit the standard profiles if you just want to tweak them slightly. In this way, your phone can adjust to the situation and regulate how quickly you chew up the battery.

**CUSTOMIZE YOUR POWER CONSUMPTION:** If you choose to create your own profiles, Power Manager has seven settings that you can fine-tune to control battery usage. The "trigger" allows you to set a condition (such as a specific battery level), and you can determine how to change the settings when the phone hits that condition.

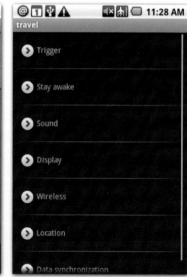

Utilities/Tools

# BatteryLife

Free
Version: 1.3.3
CurveFish

BatteryLife installs as a widget that you can access from your home screen or any other screen you put it on. To install, just tap and hold on some open real estate on your screen; when prompted, tap Widgets and select BatteryLife. Once you've added it, it will show you the amount of battery left. This simple, straightforward app doesn't manage power for you or anything like that, but it does what it should: display the status of your battery in a large, readable format.

**FOCUS ON THE TASK:** Since this is just a battery meter, you have few options to set. One nice feature is that you can set the colors of the battery icon to change as you drain your power. For example, you could set it to change from blue to yellow to bright pink as the battery goes down. That way, you don't have to squint at the status bar to tell when you're running low—the pink battery is your sign that you need to recharge.

# Battery Graph

Free
Version: 12
Morgan H

This simple graph program shows your charge over a period of time. You can export your data and see if you can figure out what's causing the biggest drain on your battery. You can also set the interval to check every five minutes or every minute, and for how many days. Use this in conjunction with Power Manager for optimal battery life.

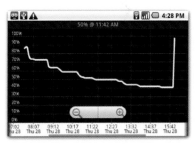

# Best App for a Custom Home Screen

## Open Home (Full)
**$3.99**
**Version: 3.8**
**Better Android**

Open Home has boatloads of themes that offer some really cool 3D looks for your home screen. Some of the best themes will set you back $0.99 each, so you might end up paying a little more than just the cost of the app. In return, you'll get some awesome customizations that take Android way beyond the defaults. For example, with Open Home you can group the apps on your home screen by type, keeping all your games in one handy place.

**EYE CANDY OR FUNCTIONALITY:** This kind of app makes your phone look really neat, but it's not just eye candy—it actually helps you find stuff on your phone. The live folder feature is truly awesome. You can earmark an app, file, RSS feed, text message, etc., to be anchored to one of your Open Home screens. This provides you with quick access to whatever you use most often. And if you've ever wondered how to take a screenshot without using the Android developer tools, this app has that ability built in.

**LIKE A SALAD BAR:** This app has a *lot* of customization options for you. Whether you want interesting fonts, an environmental look and feel, or something totally wacky, you can pretty much find the package you want or put together the pieces to make your own. You have up to seven screens to customize in whatever way you want. So if you decide to organize your apps by entertainment, communication, productivity, and lifestyle, you could earmark one screen for each.

# SlideScreen

**Free / $6.99 Full version**
**Version: 1.0.1**
**Larva Labs Ltd.**

One of the best features of an Android phone is that it is *yours*, and you can have it look and behave exactly how you want. SlideScreen lets you customize your phone to a set of preferences; for example, you can split personal and professional activities on your customized screen, separated by the weather forecast. This app will display just about anything you'd want to see, including most of the status bar items, and you can place them anywhere you want.

**YOUR LOOK AND FEEL:** Use SlideScreen's preferences to decide which items are displayed in which order. Once the app is loaded and you press the Home key, you will be prompted to decide whether to use SlideScreen or your phone's default Home. You can also set one or the other of them as your default.

# PandaHome

**Free**
**Version: 1.8.2**
**NetDragon Websoft Inc.**

PandaHome works much like Open Home, but it's a bit simpler. If you just want to add straightforward design themes to your phone, this app will do the trick. What's more, Panda-Home can load Open Home templates, so you have plenty of themes to choose from. You can switch between themes quickly by clicking the menu button and then selecting a new theme. This app is quick, easy, and polished.

# Best App for Toggling Your Settings

## Toggle Settings
Free
Version: 2.5.8
cooolmagic

Toggle Settings can instantly configure many of the settings on your phone, and it also lets you set up profiles with presets for those settings. For example, the Home profile enables data synchronization and WiFi but disables Bluetooth. You can customize this profile however you like, including adding toggles for all the settings this app can turn on and off. If you'd rather toggle settings individually, you can do that with this app as well. The profiles let you define a group of settings that are toggled all at once.

**TOGGLES AND PROFILES:** This app provides you with two toggle tabs that can have up to eight items displayed for quick selection. That's a total of up to 16 items for quick launch. In addition, you have eight profiles that modify the behavior of your phone. For example, the Charging Profile shuts down all your processes while the phone is charging up, so you get the most charge in the least time.

**PROCESS LISTS:** If you click the drop-down menu at the top of the app, you get a list of all the processes that are running. It's nice to be able to see these quickly, and also handy when you're trying to figure out what could be using your resources when you want to conserve them. From here, you can end a process, add it to the ignore list, or add it to the auto-kill list.

Utilities/Tools

# Best App to Back Up Your Files

## MyBackup Pro
**$4.99**
Version: 3.8
RerWare

Sometimes things go wrong, especially with phones. You could lose your call logs, apps, SMS history, and other types of information. But if you have a backup, it's no problem. MyBackup Pro makes a copy of all your data, so if you lose your phone, drop it in the toilet, or buy a new one, you will have all your data and apps ready to restore. MyBackup has a very simple interface and gives you five options to work with. Schedule your backups to happen when you're sleeping and you won't even know that MyBackup Pro is there...until you need it.

**SCHEDULE YOUR BACK UPS:** The scheduling feature lets you decide when to back up your data and apps. I have scheduled my SMS data to be backed up on Sunday night at 1:46 a.m. because I'm pretty sure I won't be texting at that time. I just leave my phone powered on and everything is taken care of. Once you have your backup you can view it in table format, which is easier to read than the text message itself.

**BACK UP ANYTHING:** You can back up your apps and all different kinds of data with just one click. When you schedule your backup, you can also choose to back up to the SD card or to a secure server online. If you choose to back up online, you'll have to create an account with RerWare. If you back up to an SD card, consider having one or more cards devoted only to backups, and keep them in a secure location.

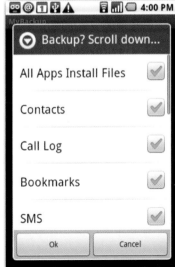

# Best App to Turn Off 3G/EDGE/GPRS

## APNDroid

**Free**
**Version: 2.0.1**
**Martin Adamek**

The next time you need to save a little battery life, use APNDroid to shut off your 3G/EDGE/GPRS data connection and prevent your apps from trying to use the network in the background. You'll still be able to make phone calls, and you can switch your data connection back on just as easily as you switched it off. You can also create a shortcut on your desktop to launch this app quickly.

**ONE CLICK:** We all like to accomplish things on our phones with just one tap, saving ourselves some time and hopefully some aggravation. APNDroid's one-click action is a quick, easy way to turn off your phone's data capabilities. Simply drag a copy of the app to your Home screen and create a shortcut to disable your Internet access in one click.

**BEST OF BOTH WORLDS:** You'll still get those important phone calls when you disable your data connection, but you won't drain your battery as fast. And if you check the option to keep MMS enabled, you'll be able to send MMS messages, even with your Internet disabled. Be forewarned, though, that if you uninstall this app while your connection is off, you'll have a hard time getting it enabled again. For more details, see *http://code.google.com/p/apndroid/*.

# Toggle Data Widget

**Free**
**Version: 2.0**
**Cameron Murphy**

This simple widget can be installed on your home screen or any other screen where you can place widgets. Once it's there, a simple click will turn your data off or on. This app also toggles the background data usage when turning WiFi on and off. Turning off data access will prevent your background processes from connecting to the network and will help save your battery.

**LEAVE MMS GOING:** Leaving MMS enabled allows you to continue to receive MMS messages even when you've got data turned off. In order to use this feature, you'll need to go into your settings (choose Wireless & Networks, Mobile Networks, then Access Point Names) and add an APN (Access Point Name) just for handling MMS.

# Network Monitor

**Free (with ads) / $0.99 Full version**
**Version: 1.6.4**
**AoB**

This is a simple tool to monitor your network connectivity. It can alert you if you are accessing too much data, which can be handy if you are roaming overseas and paying extra for data.

# Best App for Organizing Your Apps

## Apps Organizer
**Free**
**Version: 1.4.5**
**Fabio Collini**

If you're the kind of person who likes to keep everything in its proper place, you're going to love App Organizer, which lets you organize your apps into labeled groups. It comes with six standard labels, but you can create your own labels, as well and customize them however you choose. For instance, you might put all your travel apps under a label called Travel, or fill a Walking label with apps that track your location, distance, and so forth. You can also tag certain apps as favorites.

**FAVORITES:** Using the Apps tab lets you star the apps you use the most, like the most, or want to highlight for whatever reason. If you click and hold on an item, you'll be prompted to put a label on it, launch it, or uninstall it. This is pretty nice if you want quick access to your apps.

**LABELS:** Using the Labels tab takes things a step further. From here you can map a collection of apps to one label and create a shortcut to the group on one of your screens. If you find yourself filling up your screens with shortcuts and widgets, use this feature to group collections of apps together under one icon. This will help keep your screen clean and uncluttered.

# Best App for Favoring Your Apps

## UltimateFaves
**Free / $1.99 Pro version**
**Version: 2.1.1**
**Lior Gonnen**

UltimateFaves is a great tool for accessing your favorite apps with a single click. You can also flag your favorite actions, such as SMS, contacts, or dialing someone directly. The interface consists of "carousels" that can hold up to 18 items each. The free version gives you two carousels to work with; you might start out with a work carousel and a personal carousel. The Pro version allows you to install more carousels than you will ever need. I have a carousel for my most frequently SMS'd friends and another for my most used apps. It's a snap to switch quickly back and forth between carousels.

**SPIN YOUR WAY AROUND YOUR PHONE:** Carousels are an easy way to navigate through all the stuff on your phone. For applications, the carousels show each app icon, and for contacts, you'll see the picture you have associated with that person. It would be nice to be able to customize your app icons, too, but for now you just get the standard icons.

**WHEEL THROUGH YOUR ITEMS:** This app lets you map your contacts, phone numbers, email addresses, texting addresses, and browser bookmarks. One nice feature is that you can set the transparency of your items in the carousel, so you can choose whether you want it to stand out or blend into the background.

# Best App for Seeing in the Dark

## Color Flashlight

**Free**
**Version: 2.6.0**
**Social & Mobile, Inc.**

With the Color Flashlight app, you'll never be afraid of the dark again. I typically turn off all the lights in my house before I go to bed to save energy. On dark winter nights, this app helps me navigate around my house until my eyes become adjusted to the darkness. This app is all you need to get yourself around a dark, unfamiliar area, and it can be a lifesaver when the power goes out. There's even a number of cool effects and colors that you can choose from, making this app fun as well as useful.

**MIX AND MATCH:** This app offers 12 different effects and a color gradient tool that lets you select the color you would like. So, for example, if you set a base color and then select the strobe effect, you'll get whatever color you chose along with alternating black. This makes for some interesting contrasts. A word of caution: this app will wear your battery down quickly, so if you're going camping you'll want to bring a regular old flashlight along too.

**MORE EFFECTS:** Ever wish you had your own police light? This app does a pretty good imitation, and there's even a sound option to make the siren start wailing. It's loud and obnoxious, so be careful where you test it out! There are plenty of other effects, from a trippy spiral to a disco inferno.

# Best App to Navigate with a Compass

## Compass

**Free**
**Version: 1.0.22**
**Snaptic**

Like the Color Flashlight, this tool takes your device beyond typical phone stuff. As the name suggests, it provides a compass that will help you navigate your way around. Of course, you could always use Google Maps, MyTracks, or some other tracking device, but sometimes it's fun to get your bearings the old-fashioned way. This easy-to-use compass app combines the look of a classic compass with no-frills functionality. No wonder it's the number one compass app in the Android Market.

**NAVIGATE IN STYLE:** There are four main compass types to choose from: Analog, Antique, Digital, and Simple Digital. You also get three background settings: None, Sky, and Wood. On the antique compass, the needle will always point North; you obtain your directions by looking at the face of the compass.

**EASY TO GET GOING:** The Compass app offers a variety of settings to get you going quickly. If you choose Display Location, your current location will be shown on top of the compass. This pinpointed my home address on the first try, and subsequent refreshes put me within a house or two of my location. You can also set the sensor quality and determine how often the sensors update the compass heading.

# Best App for Leveling Surfaces

## Bubble

**Free**
**Version: 1.8.1**
**Ben Zibble**

Bubble is a neat tool that's been great for hanging pictures and fixing little things around my 110-year-old home. The 360 degree mode allows you to rotate an item by just the right number of degrees before you glue, nail, or tape it down. The traditional bubble level helps you get a picture or table absolutely flat or even. One cool feature is the ability to lock the measurement by tapping on the screen. There's even a voice mode that will speak any changes in your angle as they happen.

**360° MODE:** The Bubble app enables you to move an item in a 360° rotation and still keep it level. This is useful if you have to level an adjustable table or desk. Turn on the Beep and Voice mode and put the phone on top of the table. You will know when it's level, even if you've crawled underneath to adjust it.

**PRECISION IN SETTINGS:** This app gives you more than 10 settings to tweak. If you have the Text-to-Speech library installed, Bubble will speak to you when you've reached a level state. You can also have the app flash a light or buzz when it's level. Enable Tap to Lock to let you lock in the measurement when you've got it just right.

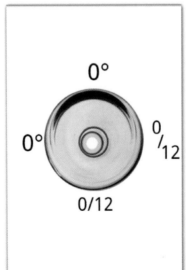

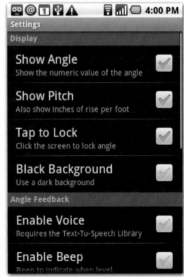

Utilities/Tools

# Best Trivial Apps

## StopWatch

**Free**
**Version: 1.3**
**Tom Taylor**

There are plenty of stopwatch apps in the Market, but I like this one the best. Its large numbers are displayed in landscape mode, and there's also a lap timer mode, which you'd expect in a stopwatch. But it also has a nice countdown feature that's great for cooking, presenting, or any event that needs to be timed. Another settings option lets you keep the screen from automatically turning off. You can also configure this app to display itself in the status bar, so you can use other apps while still keeping an eye on your timing.

**DISPLAY TIME:** Choose the Big option to enlarge the numbers and rotate the display to landscape mode. You can also select from seven different color schemes. You could use the countdown feature at an event such as Pecha Kucha or Ignite, where speakers are given a few minutes to present. An alarm could sound at the end of their time limit, so the host wouldn't have to get out the hook.

🞡 HONORABLE MENTION

## Sound Grenade

**Free**
**Version: 1.0.5**
**High Gloss**

If you really want to irritate someone, set off the Sound Grenade. It makes an incredibly annoying noise that will quickly drive someone batty. It is simple to use: just press Activate and a sound resembling an off-kilter hearing aid will begin to play. The shrill wail will annoy anyone with good hearing. When you've made your point, press Deactivate to stop the insanity.

# Best Reference Apps

Your Android device can really bail you out when you want to **answer** an elusive **question**, **identify** the **song** that's been stuck in your head, or **verify** some obscure fact that's been driving you nuts. The Android Market has many excellent apps that bring all manner of reference material to your fingertips.

Whether you are preparing to **compete** on *Jeopardy!* or your high school **debate** team, or you just want to impress your friends at parties, this chapter will help you find the apps you need. Do you know which **dictionary** works best on an Android device? What apps are best for reading **books**, **magazines**, and **newspapers**? Is there an app that will help you identify the **planets** you are seeing **in the sky**? And what kind of app can help you **order dinner in Paris,** even though you haven't spoken **French** in 20 years?

Whatever the need, there's an Android app for that, and you'll find all kinds of cool stuff in this chapter. Read on and discover some real gems.

MOTOROLA **CLIQ**™ with MOTOBLUR™

# Best App to Access Wikipedia

## Wapedia

**Free**
**Version: 1.6.1**
**Taptu**

Want to access Wikipedia from your phone with just one tap? This app makes it easy to explore the pages of Wikipedia and mark where you've been with bookmarks and a history file. This is truly a super way to navigate Wikipedia, and all the pages and headings are laid out nicely on your phone's screen. Wapedia remembers the page you were reading last, so you can pick up your research where you left off.

**INFORMATION OVERLOAD:** Wapedia lets you instantly jump from the top of a long document to the bottom. You can set a preference for how much of a page you want to load at once, and from there you can move up and down the page with arrows and intuitive navigation. This app works with other wikis , so in case you exhaust the 3 million+ articles on Wikipedia, there's tons more for you to browse.

**SHARE THE KNOWLEDGE:** If you find something wonderful, this app will let you share it quickly. Click on the Share link and you will be prompted to share via email, Facebook, or Twitter, or to open the link in a browser. Sharing ideas with friends and colleagues is a great way to strengthen social bonds and keep a conversation going. So go ahead and find, read, and share with this great resource.

## Quickpedia

Free
Version: 1.0.7
Next Mobile Web

Quickpedia is a simple app with a straightforward interface for all uses. You are given the options of Search, Featured, Popular, News, and Nearby. When a Wikipedia article is displayed on your screen, the app provides you with the options to use a Bigger Font or Smaller Font, Send to Friends, or Send to Self. You can save your email address in the settings for quick mailing in the future, and navigate to the home page by pressing the menu key and then tapping Home. You can also refresh the article, which lets you read it even when you're offline.

FEATURED AND RANDOM: This app can take you to a randomly selected article, or you can view the articles that are currently being featured on Wikipedia. Quickpedia is relegated to honorable mention status because it does not allow you to bookmark your favorite articles.

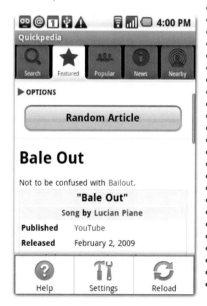

## Droid Dictionary

Free
Version: 1.4
Webcipe

This app is a simple frontend to definitions, wikis, and thesaurus entries. It includes a useful "speak" icon that will pronounce the word you are looking at. If you download the Droid Dictionary Plugin ($0.99) from the Market, you can also save your words and definitions with this app.

# More Apps to Access Wikipedia

 **HONORABLE MENTION**

## WikiMobile Encyclopedia

**Free**
**Version: 1.2.1**
**Bonfire Media, Inc.**

This app deserves recognition for being somehow faster to use than a web interface. I'm not sure how they did this, but WikiMobile Encyclopedia is super-fast and easy to use. It scrolls left to right, like a book. Pressing the Quick Facts button allows you to skip right to the most important details on a topic, displaying a short summary that's perfect for viewing on a small device like a phone. This saves you from scrolling page after page through the whole article when all you need is a basic rundown. There's even an animation of a dog chasing his tail to amuse you as you wait for results.

**DRAWN TO RANDOM:** I find myself drawn to the Random Article feature—it's a great way to gain new knowledge every day. This app also brings the most popular articles to the forefront, and puts your bookmarks front and center for easy access. Bookmarks are easy to set and remove; simply press the menu key when you are on an article you want to bookmark.

**MAKE A SLIDESHOW:** If you're reading an article with plenty of images and want to view them all in one go, you can simply click the menu key, choose Images, and sit back and watch a slideshow of all the article's images. This is a nice feature when you are looking at biology articles and others with high concentrations of images.

# Wikidroid

**Free**
**Version: 1.5**
**Sirius Applications, Ltd.**

This is a good alternative to Wapedia and does the important things well: page layouts are nicely formatted for your device, and the search and share functions are easy to use. It's important to keep your results organized and sharable when you're dealing with such a large repository of information. One fun feature is the random content shuffler, which can bring you interesting information that you wouldn't even have thought to look for. It's a great way to learn something new every day of the year.

**BASICS DONE WELL:** WikiDroid was built as a frontend for Wikipedia, so its functionality is pretty basic. The Bookmarks feature is very nice, but lacks a history file. The only preference you need to set is your language. This app is simple and easy to use, and does a good job of formatting the Mobile Wikipedia site for your phone.

# WikiTap

**Free**
**Version: 0.7**
**Veveo Inc.**

This is a nice interface to Wikipedia articles that will also lead you to videos on the subject. Any available videos related to the article you're viewing will be displayed across the bottom of your screen, adding another layer to your understanding of the topic and saving you from having to do a separate YouTube search. This app also gives you the option to format the page, read the regular web version, or see a table of contents. With a quick tap of your finger, you can also hide any of the videos you come across, which can be handy if you get something unexpected in your search results.

# Best Dictionary App

## Free Dictionary Org

**Free**
**Version: 2.0**
**Baris Efe**

We all need a dictionary sometimes, whether it's to find the meaning of a word or to confirm its spelling. This app's killer feature is the automatic suggestions that appear as you type. After all, if you don't know how to spell a word, you need a little help finding it in the first place! What's more, once you've looked up a word, you can copy it to a note where you can annotate it or add a picture. And if you speak other languages, you can load multiple dictionaries from the Market.

**TYPE A LITTLE:** Some words are tough to spell. (For some people, a *lot* of words are tough to spell.) With this app, you can just type part of the word and your list will start to fill up. You can then choose the word you're looking for. This app is a lifesaver if you want to find a word and drill down into its meaning. You can also have a word spoken to you, so when you think you hear someone butcher a word, you can confirm your suspicions before you gently correct them.

**ANNOTATE AWAY:** The annotation feature works with the 3Banana Notes app, which I highly recommend you install. Then, you can tap the plus sign next to the word in Free Dictionary and you'll be taken to 3Banana Notes, where you can mark up the definition, take a picture or attach one that you already have, and make the word your own. You can also use tags so you can find your notes of defined words easily. The combination of Free Dictionary and 3Banana Notes is an invaluable addition to your phone.

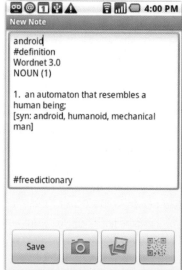

# WordMate

**Free**
**Version: 1.2**
**Hongbo**

One of WordMate's most powerful features is its ability to load extra dictionaries. You can load dictionaries for both your primary and secondary language, as well as a thesaurus. Having multiple dictionaries can also be invaluable if you work in a field with its own particular jargon. For example, the Dictionary of Computing contains technical terms that we deal with here at O'Reilly every day. Unfortunately, newer terms like Cloud and Web 2.0 aren't included yet—maybe we'll have to build an O'Reilly Dictionary that you can plug into WordMate!

**SELECT YOUR PREFERENCE:** There are eight standard dictionaries available from the Market, and takes just a tap to load one onto your phone. Once you have all your dictionaries loaded, it's a snap to choose one to work with. This app will become better and better as more specialized dictionaries become available.

# Quick Dictionary

**Free**
**Version: 1.0.1**
**Lorenzo Colitti**

Quick Dictionary is a simple app that looks up words using *dict.org*. No fancy bells, whistles, or settings, but the app works well and takes up very little disk space. The only catch is that it requires you to be online.

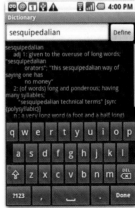

# Best Thesaurus App

## English Thesaurus Dictionary
**Free**
**Version: 1.0.9**
**Notes**

If you're forever searching for just the right word to communicate your meaning, this is the app you need. It even helps you spell out words if you don't know exactly what you're looking for and keeps a history of all the words you look up. This can save you time if there are certain words you use all the time and yet can't quite keep in your head. Why keep typing the same thing and trying in vain to remember something if the app remembers for you? I really like this app. Or should I say, I *strongly relish* this app.

**EXCELLENT FUNCTIONALITY:** If you often use this app to search for words, you'll build up a history file that shows you all the words you've looked up and how many times you've accessed a particular word. This is very useful, as you can start to see patterns in your word usage. For example, I tend to look for precision words that add more clarity to my writing, and my daughter looks for replacement words so she does not repeat herself too much.

 **HONORABLE MENTION**

## Thesaurus Free
**Free / €.99 Full version**
**Version: 1.1.1**
**SpeedyMarks**

This simple thesaurus brings back quick results. Each result is itself a link, and when clicked will bring back still more different yet related words. This gives you a quick way to explore words that are similar in meaning to what you're looking for, but not exactly the same. The free version has quite a few ads, so if you're bothered by that, pony up the €0.99 and purchase the full version.

Reference

# Best App to Listen to NPR News

## NPR News

**Free**
**Version: 1.1RC1**
**NPR**

If you're a National Public Radio junkie who scans the low 90s on the radio whenever you're in a car, this is an app you need. You'll be able to access all the great programming available on NPR, plus many of the written articles found on NPR.org. So whether you are looking to hear the top stories of the day or listen to your favorite programs, such as *Fresh Air, On Point, All Things Considered, Talk of the Nation, Wait, Wait Don't Tell Me,* or *This American Life,* this app lets you tune in even when you're nowhere near a radio.

**SCHEDULE YOUR LISTENING:** Like most people, you probably spend most of your day rushing around. So in those rare moments when you find yourself alone with just your phone, you can fire up this app and listen to your favorite NPR program. If you want to access the unique programming found on the local NPR channels, you can search for stations by call letters or zip code.

**MAKE YOUR PLAYLIST:** Do you love a certain NPR program but never have time to listen to it when it's on? Make a playlist with all your favorite shows. When you browse programs and click on the show you want, you have the option to listen to it right then and there or add it to a playlist. When you finally have some time to kill, fire up this app and listen to your playlist.

213

# Best Electronic Book Reader

## Aldiko
**Free / $1.99 Full version**
**Version: 1.2.6.1**
**Aldiko Limited**

Who needs another expensive device dedicated to just reading books when you already have your Android phone with you? Aldiko gets mobile book reading right, with an eye-pleasing, customizable format (by font, color, margins, etc.). You can curl up with your favorite books or take them on the go. Aldiko will read any ePub file, which you can import yourself or download through Aldiko's online catalog. (Many O'Reilly Media titles are available in ePub format from oreilly.com.)

**OFF THE SHELF:** The attractive dashboard that greets you when Aldiko launches gives you quick access to your recently read books, your whole eBook library, and a portal to a variety of catalogs where you can download new books. Just choose a new book to read, or pick up an old one from wherever you left off. With one click of the menu button you can search your library for the title you are looking for.

**BROWSE THE CATALOG:** Aldiko taps into a variety of sources for discovering both free and paid books that are available to download. Feedbooks.com is a great place to find free books, both original content and classic works culled from the public domain. Specialized catalogs include technical content from O'Reilly eBooks, romance novels from All Romance eBooks, and books by independent authors and publishers distributed by Smashwords.

Reference

# WordPlayer

**Free**
**Version: v3**
**Word-Player Team**

WordPlayer lets you choose from millions of books that are available from free and public domain sources. You can choose from Google Books, Smashwords, Feedbooks, Movies, Classics, Banned Books, The Oz Books, and more. You can also load books from your SD card if you have obtained them elsewhere, or you can use Calibre Libre and wirelessly transfer books from your desktop or laptop to your phone. This great app earns a strong honorable mention.

**ESTABLISH/ORGANIZE YOUR LIBRARY:**
This app has three simple ways to organize your library: by Subjects, Authors, or Cover View. You can search and sort books according to these three views, and also bookmark any sections you like so you can quickly navigate to the spot later. Another nice feature is the ability to preview a book before you download.

# FBReader

**Free**
**Version: v3**
**Geometer Plus**

If you've already purchased ePub, oeb, or bb2 (*.zip*) files you can put them in the Books directory of your SD card and read them with FBReader. Use your USB to connect your computer to your phone, and you'll be able to copy files over easily.

strategy. Failure to select and communicate a single strategy creates significant additional hurdles to success. The MurderBoarding process provides a way for teams to evaluate ideas against the beliefs, needs, and capabilities of the organization. The process itself is about simplifying requirements, views, and knowledge to make decisions, and then enriching the understanding more deeply so that the ultimate choice is well thought through. An organizational testing component is included in the

# Best Periodical Reader

## Issuu Mobile

**Free**
**Version: 1.0.0**
**Issuu**

Your eBook reader handles your novels and nonfiction books perfectly, but it's useless with the shorter-form and more ephemeral stuff of magazines and newspapers. For that, Issuu Mobile is a good start, offering a great interface for reading magazines, getting news feeds, organizing a periodical library, and managing subscriptions. Its selection is somewhat limited at the moment, but the technology is developed well enough that it could eventually become your go-to digital newsstand.

**DIGITAL NEWSSTAND:** Browse through Issuu's categories to get an idea of what's available, and check out the handy Featured tab to see what's hot and recommended by Issuu. This app also shows you what the community of users has rated highest.

**COLOPHON:** Get details on every periodical, including length, date published, a description, and comments from previous readers. You can bookmark an issue for later, subscribe to future issues, or share an issue with your contacts. If you like what you're reading, you can also find related magazines or newspapers.

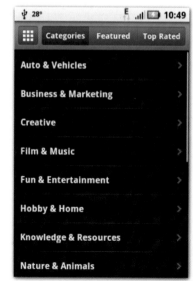

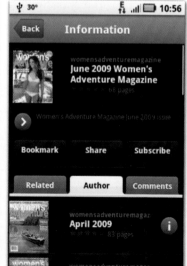

**PAGE BY PAGE**: Once you start reading some magazine articles, you'll begin to understand why it's so much more difficult to present graphically rich media like this as opposed to just simple text. Layout is important, and you'd lose something in the translation if an article were stripped down to just its text. Full-page view is great for navigation and for flipping through pages or sections, but it's not so hot for reading.

**SCRATCH THAT**: Thankfully, Issuu does a good job of giving you the best of both full-page contextual aesthetics and readability. When reading in full-page view, just "scratch" the surface (touch and drag a box) to highlight the selection you want to read and magnify it on the screen.

**MORE READABLE**: After "scratching" the surface, you'll be much better able to read the magnified view of the section you just highlighted. You'll even see a thumbnail view of the passage in context, reminding you of where you are in the article. Scroll down or over for more, or select the Back button to zoom in on a different section.

# Best Bible App

## Bible
**Free**
Version: 2.0
LifeChurch.tv

There are more than 20 English-language translations of the Bible, including the American Standard Version, the Amplified Bible, and the King James Version. This app includes all of these and more, packing a total of more than 27 translations. If you are currently studying the Bible, you will find what you need in this app. The ability to create bookmarks is very handy, and if you create a YouVersion account, you can sync your reading with your desktop computer and phone.

**SPREAD THE WORD:** When you tap and hold on a particular verse, you'll be prompted to select Bookmark, Share, Contributions, Copy, or Clear Section. Selecting Contributions will take you to a list of what others have said about the passage. It's interesting to read how other people put different passages into context in today's world. If you decide to share, you will be asked which of your communication tools you want to use.

**STUDY PLAN:** If you participate in a Bible study group, you may want to select one of the plans that comes bundled in this app. The plans guide you in your study of the Bible, and their timelines vary from one month to two years. Each plan suggests an appropriate amount of daily reading material—about 20 minutes per day. To understand and digest everything in the Bible will likely take a lifetime, and this app can assist you on your journey.

# Best App to Get Your Facts Straight

## Useless Facts

**Free**
**Version: 3.7**
**Qorona**

Ever met someone who seems to know everything about everything? Maybe they're a genius, but maybe they just used this app and filled their cranium with a bunch of Useless Facts. This app is addictive—once you start scrolling through, you'll come across items that will shock, entertain, amaze, and enlighten you. You'll like the ability to email the fact or send it via SMS message. You can also set this app's border, background, and text colors.

**SHARE THE USELESSNESS:** Once you find a fact that you like, click "share" and your newfound useless tidbit will be queued up for sending via text message or email. Each time you run the app, the useless facts are freshly shuffled so you don't end up reading the same facts in order.

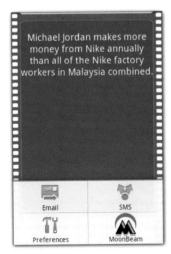

**HONORABLE MENTION**

## 9000+ Awesome Facts

**Free**
**Version: 4.0**
**Shrav B. Mehta**

If you have some time to kill and you prefer facts to fiction, get this app and have some fun. Like the previous app, it can get addictive as you scroll through fact after fact, or pick one random fact after another. You can also share the facts you find using email or SMS.

# Best Speech Translator App

## Talk To Me

Free
Version: 1.1.3
Flaviu Negrean

This is a great tool for learning the basics of another language or for communicating with someone who does not speak your language. This app can translate between spoken Spanish, French, German, Italian, and English (UK or U.S.). (Other languages are available for written translation.) This nifty tool will serve you well when you are in a restaurant and want to know the specials. Not only that, but you can order your meal in style, too, since you can also hear how to say it. What traditional phrasebook can do that?

**TRAVEL ASSISTANT:** Want to be more independent while traveling? Get this app and quit walking around asking people if they speak English. You can change your language settings from the main screen or in the settings.

**WORDS ARE NO PROBLEM:** With this app it's easy to have a text conversation with someone who speaks another language. Simply use the swap feature found in the Settings section of the Menu tab to quickly switch from primary language to secondary language. This allows you to keep the conversation going smoothly because it takes just one click to switch languages and one more click to text the result.

Reference

# Best Speech and Text Translator App

## Google Translate

Free
Version: 1.0.25
Google

This is a great tool, both for learning to speak small phrases of another language and for finding dictionary-like definitions for the words you type in. You can choose from more than 46 languages. Possibly the best feature of this app is the ability to simply click on the audio icon to hear the word spoken. You can also see your history and any translated words and phrases that you've saved (useful if you find yourself always asking for directions or looking for a restroom). *Apreciar!*

**PRACTICE YOUR SPEAKING:** Practicing pronunciation is an invaluable part of learning another language. Related Phrases is another cool feature that puts the word you are looking for in the context of commonly used phrases. This is a great way to learn a couple of phrases quickly. This app also provides a definition of the word in question, so you'll know that you're using it correctly.

 **HONORABLE MENTION**

## Trippo

Free
Version: 1.0.2
Cellictica

As its name suggests, Trippo is designed specifically for travelers. This app can translate and speak words and phrases from more than 20 languages; many more languages are available in the written form only. You can send the results to friends via SMS, email, Facebook, and other methods.

# Best App for Avoiding Traffic Snarls

## Augmented Traffic Views
**Free**
**Version: 1.1.0**
**Augmented Views**

This augmented reality app is a great way to see what the traffic is like in the large metropolitan areas covered by this app. It's extremely gratifying to view ugly traffic snarls that you cleverly managed to avoid. Another neat feature is the preloaded Points of Interest (POIs). (You can also create your own custom POIs if you're up for a little hacking.) Additionally, you can overlay Phantom POIs that will alert you of speed cameras, red light cameras, and other alerts from PhantomAlerts.com. But you don't need that, because you're carefully obeying all the traffic laws. Right?

**RADAR VIEW:** This totally cool view uses Google Maps and live data from your state and local city. As more and more government bodies see the importance of apps like this, more data will become available. And with more data will come more great apps.

**REAL ON THE MAP:** This app offers a number of different views. There's a base Google Map, then local traffic is layered on top of that, and if you click Augmented Traffic View, your camera will insert your vehicle into the scene. How cool is that? Create points of interest to map your route home and you'll see what's ahead before you approach it. Very handy on a snow day in New England.

I-93 at Sullivan Square (Exit 28) (3.1

# Best App to Contact Congress

## Congress

Free
Version: 1.5.3
Sunlight Labs

This app from the Sunlight Foundation shines a new light on your local legislators. You can find the legislators that are closest to your GPS location or search for them by state, by zip code, or by their last names. You can see which committees they serve on, and if there are any news items, Twitter tweets, or YouTube videos about them out there. This is a great tool to help you understand who is making decisions for your state. You also get phone numbers and websites for each member of Congress. This is a handy app for those who want to get involved, rather than just complain about a lack of progress.

**DON'T LET 'EM HIDE:** There are several ways to track down your legislators and give them a piece of your mind. Be aware that searching by last name is an exact science. Because there is no autocomplete feature, you need to spell the last name exactly right.

**FIND THEM ANYWHERE:** You may wonder just who else is on the committees that your legislator serves on. With this app you can simply click on the committee to see a list of all the members. You can then drill down to see each member's Profile, News, Tweets, and YouTube videos. I understand that a future update to this app will include voting records too, so the next time someone is giving a political speech, you'll be able to do your own fact-checking with your phone.

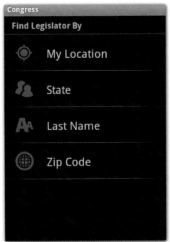

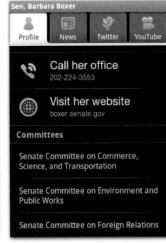

# Best App for Galaxy Gazing

## Google Sky Map
**Free**
**Version: 1.3**
**Google**

This is the first app that our 12-year-old installed on his Android phone, and he continues to use it alongside his telescope. When the app is in automatic mode, you can move your phone in different directions and the planets, stars, constellations, and heavenly objects will come into focus. This allows you to get a more precise view than what your telescope likely offers, assuming you aren't using the Hubble. The brightness of the objects on your screen are the same as what you see in the sky, so next time you see a bright star on the horizon, find out which one it is.

**KNOW WHAT YOU WANT TO SEE:** If you know what star or planet you want to view, use the search feature to have the app tell you which way to point your phone. The object you're looking for will appear on your screen in the crosshairs, as shown in the upper-right hand corner below. As you move your phone in the direction of the object, a big yellow circle will surround it and let you know you've found your target. The color of the circle around the arrow changes from cold colors to warm colors as you get closer.

**NIGHT MODE:** The red color used in night mode is designed to keep your eyes adapted to the darkness. Tapping the screen will cause the control panel to appear on the left side. This panel allows you to toggle several settings on and off: Stars, Constellations, Messier Objects, Planets, Grid Lines, and Horizon layers. This can come in handy if you find your screen is getting too crowded. Zoom in by tapping the screen again and bringing up the magnification icon.

Reference

# Best Earth Clock App

## TerraTime

**Free 14-day trial / $2.50 Full version**
**Version: 1.3**
**Udell Enterprises**

TerraTime is not only visually attractive, it packs some real power below the surface. It offers settings for location awareness, the ability to have the earth view loaded as a live background on your screen, and more. There are options for viewing in map mode, time mode, or earth view. Once you have the settings how you like them, install TerraTime as your home screen. You're then able to flip between screens and see what the world looks like from space at that very moment, right from your phone.

**TURN ON THE LIGHTS:** The globe view allows you to see where the sun is shining on the earth. The polar ice caps are included in the view below; you can also choose to include all the stars in the background. Or view the world in a map mode, with layers of clouds, stars, etc. The first time you load this app, make sure you have a fast connection, because the images are high-resolution pics from NASA that take some time to download.

**CLOCK MODE:** The clock option provides almanac information such as sunrise and sunset and how long the days are. The clock also shows moonrise and moonset, the phases of the moon, what time the stars will be visible, and how many hours of darkness/light there will be. The moon is represented by a gray line showing when it will be visible in the sky.

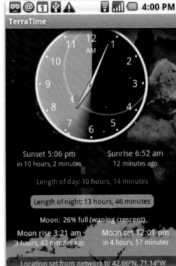

# QR Code Index

1001 Cocktails, 107

8 Footprints, 101

9000+Awesome-Facts, 219

A Online Radio, 140

A World of Photo, 11

aContacts, 38

ActionComplete, 119

Advanced Task Killer, 189

aiMinesweeper, 161

Air Hockey, 159

AKNotepad, 36

Aldiko, 214

Alice (Gig Guide), 139

ALOQA, 60

Amazon.com, 51

AndExplorer, 41

AndFTP, 43

Android Finance, 59

Android Terminal Emulator, 187

Andrometer, 33

Any Cut, 184

AnyPost, 88

Apartments, 110

APNDroid, 196

Apps Organizer, 198

Astrid, 118

aTrackDog, 188

AudioManager Widget, 133

DroidDrop, 46

Dungeon Quest, 173

EasyMoney, 52

eBuddy, 76

English Thesaurus Dictionary, 212

EStrongs File Exporer, 40

Evernote, 37

Facebook for Android, 90

Fandango Movies, 127

Faves, 84

Favorite Recipes, 106

FBReader, 215

FeedRNews Reader, 92

Financisto, 53

Find Green, 102

FireWallet, 54

FoxyRing, 20

Free Dictionary Org, 210

Fun Towers, 175

FxCamera, 23

Gem Miner, 160

Gmote, 132

GoAruna, 46

Google Sky Map, 224

Google Translate, 221

Google Voice, 83

GPSCaddy, 34

Graviturn Extended, 15

Handcent SMS, 73

HelloTXTroid, 89

Hoccer, 24

iBird Explorer Pro, 122

iNap: Arrival Alert, 30

Issuu Moble, 216

Jamendo Player, 141